MW01489112

Contents

This book is dedicated to all the people in my life who have given me the loving words I needed when I wasn't able to find them myself. Most notably, Sheida, Skye, and Cinta – you are the ultimate power-women who have the unique ability to validate without placating and to empathize whilst empowering. Rather than telling me to "stay strong" or "cheer up", you have always been able to listen, validate, and let me be in whatever it is I am feeling, helping me to navigate these moments with love.

That allowance is a liferaft that helps us to stay afloat in the face of sinking into the challenging moments. It is through hearing all of these loving words I needed from others that I learned how to give it to myself; being able to become my own liferaft when I need it.

Now, in hopes of paying it forward, my wish is that these words keep you afloat, dear reader. So you can not only feel supported to be exactly as you are, but to learn how to give yourself this, and to understand that you had the power, all along, to receive all the loving words you've ever needed – *from yourself.*

This Is For You

The words you will read here are all the loving words you might need.

Sometimes, they'll be soft love.

Sometimes, tough love.

Sometimes, it'll be purely validating your struggles.

And sometimes, you'll hear some thoughts that may help you see things another way.

Read these words as YOU speaking to YOU.

In reality, the loving space within you, which perhaps you haven't heard from in a long time (or ever), wants to say this.

These words express the truth of what you really know, deep down underneath the patterns of self-protection and self-criticism that we have learned over our lifetime.

The words are true.

Your body knows them.

Even if your mind does not fully believe them yet.

Read them slowly.

Be gentle.

Let these words wash over you.

Encourage you.

Pick you up on days when you feel like the best you can do is fall into a puddle onto the floor.

It's okay.

How you feel it is okay.

Even if you don't believe the words, just hold a space that maybe, just maybe, something deeper within you is letting them sink in.

Allow yourself to revisit the pages again and again as you need.

You deserve to hear these words.

You deserve all the love that your inner self wants to give you.

You are deserving.

Of all the loving words you need.

So, here they are...

You Are Enough

It's easy to get lost in the idea that you're not doing enough. That you need to be more. That you need to prove yourself. That you need to add, take away, or change yourself in order to be worthy.

That in order to feel enough, you need to first earn it.

Read these next words very carefully.

You are enough. Right now. As you are.

Yes – **flaws and all.** Shortcomings and all.

You don't have to do more, be more, or change anything. You're already worthy of love, peace, connection, joy, and success.

I know you might feel like you have to fix something first to be deserving of your enoughness.

It's not true. You don't. We live in a world that makes us constantly compare ourselves to others. Social media, the people around us, pressures and expectations we place on ourselves, and even our own thoughts can convince us that we're falling short.

But the reality is, you're doing just fine.

You're here, you're trying, and that is what matters.

Even if you don't feel like you are trying right now, you are enough. Yes, laying on the floor doing nothing at all, you are enough. Making mistakes, you are enough. Not showing up perfectly, you are still enough.

You don't have to do it all at once. You don't have to be everything for everyone. You don't have to become worthy by chasing, changing, and controlling... You are worthy now. Right now.

Just showing up is enough.

Want to fall into your bed and hide from the world? You are still enough. Want to scream at the top of your lungs because you're so incredibly frustrated? You are still enough. Feel guilty about the way you acted in the past? Yep, you guessed it, **you are enough.**

Even when you revisit all the things you've done that you believe are mistakes. Even when you remember all the ways you "failed" yourself or someone else. Even in your darkness.

You. Are. Still. Enough. Remember that. Say it over and over. Feel the truth of it settle into our cells.

It's Okay Not To Be Okay

Sometimes, life feels heavy. Maybe a little heavy. Maybe the-weight-of-the-world-heavy.

It's okay. Even when you feel so utterly not okay.

It's okay.

You're not alone if you feel the pressure to keep it together, to act like you've got it all figured out.

Give yourself a break. You're human. You're allowed to struggle. You're allowed to not be okay. It doesn't make you weak.

The irony is that it feels even heavier when we try to pretend it's not heavy.

Why do we pretend things are lighter than they are?

We want them to be lighter, so out of sheer will, we gloss over the heavy feels and skip to the lightness that we know deep down we'll eventually feel again.

But it doesn't work. Skipping over the heavy can make it even heavier. It's understandable, and it's easy for us to be afraid of not being okay. Maybe you don't know if it's actually okay to not be okay. Maybe you were never allowed to not be okay.

It doesn't feel good. I know. But it really is okay to not be okay. You're safe to feel heavy. Let yourself feel what you feel. You don't need to tell yourself to "cheer up" or to "stay strong" right now.

You're safe to be struggling right now.

You're allowed to not have it together. You're allowed to fall to the ground. You're allowed to feel like a mess.

You don't have to hide behind a smile or pretend that everything's fine. Not here. All parts of you are welcome here. It's okay to have tough (or intensely horrible) days, weeks, months, or years. You don't need to fix everything right now.

Fall apart, take a break, and let yourself feel what you're feeling. You're allowed to not have it all together. You've been through a lot, and it's understandable that you feel overwhelmed.

Let yourself be overwhelmed. You don't even have to try to get through it right now.

You can just be. Be here. In whatever is there.

Give yourself permission to be exactly where you are.

It's okay not to be okay.

You Deserve To Be Heard

You deserve to be heard. Your voice matters.

There's nothing too trivial that you have to say. Whatever you need to express, it deserves to be heard and respected. It might feel silly to say it aloud, but if it feels right, then let yourself speak it.

You are worthy of sharing your thoughts, your feelings, your struggles, your ideas, and your dreams. You don't have to stay silent or keep your thoughts to yourself. It's easy to believe the story that to be accepted or understood, we have to stay silent. You're not alone in thinking that people will prefer you if you were agreeable and "easy going."

But are those the people who truly want to connect with?

How would it feel to be accepted, embraced, and respected for your raw, honest messy truth? To have people who support you in your unique way of looking at life...

To surround yourself with people that don't push you away for feeling what you feel, or for being confused and imperfect. What a relief it would be to be able to let go of trying to always say the right thing and, instead, just let yourself be yourself 100%.

You deserve to express yourself, to speak up, and to make your needs known, and to own your uniqueness.

Your ideas and your emotions are valuable, and they deserve to be acknowledged. Don't shrink back any longer. Don't silence yourself just to make others comfortable. If people prefer your silence, they're not the people for you.

You're not here to please everyone. And you won't, anyway. Plus, that's not even where peace and fulfillment are found. You're not going to feel uplifted and happy by silencing yourself. Those connections you create based on sharing only part of who you are.

By dimming your light, quieting your voice, and editing yourself, they're not real connections that are being made anyway. They're connections based on a false version of yourself.

It's that false version connecting with them, not actually YOU. You're here to be authentic. To be you. All of you. Whatever you have to say.

And sometimes, that means speaking your truth, even when it's hard. Sometimes that does also mean silence, but not because you have to be, but because that is the most true for you.

So, speak up. Your voice is worth listening to. And we are listening.

You are worth being listened to. *You deserve to be heard.*

Take A Deep
Breath

Take a deep breath. Right now.

You know that feeling... When everything starts to feel like it's coming at you all at once? When you feel like you can't catch up. Like you are stuck on a hamster wheel that's going 100 miles an hour...

Take a deep breath. Right now.

I know life feels overwhelming. There's a lot to do. So much that you feel. An insurmountable amount to figure out. But just pause all of that for a moment. Let's hit that mute button.

Take a deep breath. Right now.

Your body is trying to tell you to slow down.

Take a deep breath. Right now. Even if everything feels out of control, even if you feel like you're falling apart – just stop for a moment. Breathe.

In through your nose. Hold it for a second. Now, let it out slowly. Feel your body release a little bit of the tension. It's simple, but it works. Sometimes, the most simple thing is exactly what was always needed. You don't need a perfect plan, you don't need all the answers right now. You just need to pause.

Take a deep breath. Right now.

You deserve to take a moment for yourself. You don't need to do anything else to earn this breath. You deserve to breathe. In this moment, you don't have to be on the go. You don't have to be perfect. Just breathe, and give yourself permission to be where you are.

Take a deep breath. Right now.

You'll get back to everything, but first, take a deep breath. You're doing just fine (even if it doesn't feel like it).

Go ahead. Take a deep breath. Enjoy it. And know that it's always there for you to come back to.

Your Ideas
Matter

You deserve to have your ideas heard and respected.

Your ideas are valuable. Your dreams, goals, thoughts, opinion – *they matter.* Each and every one of them. If you've not shared your ideas because you don't believe they'll be accepted or appreciated, it's time to tell yourself a new story.

Your ideas do matter. And you first need to really let yourself feel and believe that. You deserve to create an environment where you feel supported to share your ideas, and know that they won't be rejected.

That starts with not rejecting them yourself. Give yourself time and space to dream up the wildest dreams. To let yourself imagine all of the ways life could look, and what you could create.

Validate your own ideas, and know that others will, too. Maybe not everyone. And maybe not the certain people you would love to validate your ideas. That is sad, and okay that it might make you feel a little disappointed. But just because someone else might seem to not care so much about your ideas, doesn't mean you should toss them aside, too.

That's where you're needed to be your own best cheer-leader. Your own best supporter. And to start creating relationships with others who affirm that, too. They are out there, and they are ready to give you all the support and all of the listening that you would love to receive.

When you give yourself the validation, you start to attract people in your life who do, too. If you keep listening to your self-doubt, telling yourself your ideas won't matter, you will allow relationships into your life where your ideas don't matter to others.

If you're treating yourself that way, and accepting that treatment, you'll accept it from others, too.

It's time now to believe that your ideas matter and to hold this truth gently, but strongly. Your ideas are not too small. They're not too out there. They're not too insignificant. You are not too inexperienced or too young or too whatever to have ideas that are worth something. Every thought, every vision, every spark of creativity that comes to you has power.

Just because the world isn't always listening, doesn't mean your ideas aren't important. You have the power to place importance on your ideas and to listen to yourself.

The world needs fresh perspectives. It needs your voice, your spin on things, and your unique approach. Your ideas have the potential to change things – big or small.

They don't need to be fully fleshed out, and they certainly don't need to look like anyone else's ideas. Also, remember that they will never be perfect ideas. No idea ever is. That doesn't mean it can't be a brilliant idea.

You don't need anyone's permission to believe in your ideas. You don't need to wait for a sign or approval. Your ideas are worth pursuing just because they are *yours*.

Don't let anyone make you feel like your ideas are not worth acting on (including yourself). They are, and they will lead you somewhere. Even if that is simply your own satisfaction.

Your ideas matter. Own them. Nurture them. Let them grow.

You Don't Have
To Be Perfect

Read that again.

I know it feels like you have to be perfect. That pressure that you feel is understandably heavy. It's an intense weight to carry, trying to be perfect all of the time. But you really don't have to.

It's not even possible to be perfect. It's a made-up ideal that eats away at your happiness and uniqueness.

Sure, you could keep trying to reach perfection. *But do you really want to?* Trying to be perfect is exhausting. It drains our energy, and makes us feel like we've failed when we wake up, yet again, not perfect. Not reaching those unreachable standards is an energy killer. Key word there: **unreachable.**

Even if we "reach" what we define as perfect, the next task usually set for ourselves is to then "maintain" the perfection. And in a world where everything is constantly changing; where there is light, dark, and mistakes that come with being human, the maintenance of perfection will always fall short.

It's okay to make mistakes. It's okay to not have it all figured out. It's okay to not be where you thought you would. Where you want to be. You're not a robot; you're human.

And for good reason. Robots are boring AF.

Perfection is a trap. This unattainable standard makes us feel like we're constantly failing. And somehow, everyone else seems to be able to reach perfection. You must be doing something wrong...

But is that really true?

Nope. No one is perfect. Even the ones who seem to have it all figured out – spoiler alert – they don't.

Chances are, they feel the exact same as you. We're all just trying our best, figuring things out as we go. You don't have to be flawless to be loved or worthy. You don't have to be perfect to earn fulfillment and happiness.

Perfection is overrated. Being you is way more interesting. Being you actually allows you to grow. Not because you want to be perfect but because it feels good to grow at whatever pace feels right.

How are you supposed to enjoy the yumminess of growing, expanding, and advancing in different parts of life if you're already perfect?

You've done things that you thought you couldn't do. You've survived things you didn't think you'd make it through. You've felt a deep peace. Expansive joy. Love. Those moments didn't require perfection. They required you to simply be yourself. That's all anyone can ask for.

What if you stopped holding yourself to a standard that doesn't even exist? How would that feel? *Would it feel like an exhale to your soul?* It's okay to be messy and to fall short. You're allowed to be imperfect. You're allowed to be human.

Perfection isn't real. But you? You're real. And that's more than enough.

It's Okay If You Don't Feel Successful

Feel like everyone else has all the things you want? Why does it seem like they've got all the good luck? How come the answers and the accomplishments just fall into their lap?

Firstly, remember that no ones journey to success is a straight line, and most of what we see is curated and just a tiny glimpse of the journey. While it's true that some people are lucky, it doesn't mean they don't have their own challenges and struggles.

Success is such a subjective thing; what feels like a great success to one person will feel like a small, normal thing to another. What you want will be different from what others want. What is huge for them could be little for you. What is a great achievement for you could be something that others don't really want.

The point is, your definition of success is unique, and it will always move and shift. We will reach one goal and create another. And then, on the way to one goal we realize we want something else and shift our direction. That will happen in life again and again, and if we accepted the ever-changing nature of success, that would give every single person a lot more peace.

If you don't feel successful right now, that's okay. It's normal to feel that way, and it doesn't make you unworthy of it. It doesn't make you less valuable as a person. It doesn't make you incapable or weak.

It doesn't even make you an unsuccessful person – that is simply a definition and a label that you can choose to give to yourself or not.

It's easy to think you're falling short when you look around and see what others have, or what you think you should have by now. But success isn't about meeting someone else's expectations or ticking off boxes. It's okay to not feel like you've "made it."

What's important is that you don't believe in these stories and definitions too much. They can keep you locked into feeling bad or unworthy. They can make you feel stuck, even if you are moving forward. They can dampen your happiness and enjoyment of your journey on the way to your goals. And what's the point of reaching a goal if you're not even present to all the time you spend reaching it? You'd let your own life fly by you without realizing it.

Success isn't this fixed point you're supposed to hit. It's not a label, a number, or an achievement that magically defines you.

I know we've been led to believe that; and it doesn't take away from the great feeling of reaching a goal – enjoy those moments because they're wonderful to celebrate. It's just important for us to remind ourselves that we aren't defined by our success (or "lack" of it).

Success really doesn't have to look any certain way. It's okay if it looks different for you or if it hasn't quite clicked yet into the picture you imagine. You don't have to have all the pieces perfectly lined up to be happy and fulfilled in life.

It's okay if you don't feel like you're there yet. However long it takes, it's about enjoying your time here – every single day – whether you meet the goals or not.

Your worth isn't attached to a timeline. Your worth isn't based on how much you've done or how fast you've done it. What you've done, or haven't done, doesn't take away from who you are. There's no shame in not feeling "successful." It's just a feeling, and it doesn't define you. And like all feelings, it will change.

You're allowed to be in a space where things are still unfolding. You're allowed to question if you're on the right path. You're allowed to take your time. You're allowed to stop and start again. To change your mind and try something else.

You're living, learning, and growing at your own pace. Own that! Own your path, whether it gets you to the success you're imagining or not.

P.S. Another tip is to redefine success for yourself. Perhaps tapping into inner peace throughout the day is success. Maybe giving yourself kind, loving words when you used to give yourself criticism is success. Or even working towards living a more happiness-led life is where you'll find your success.

Your Insecurities Are Welcome

You don't have to hide your insecurities.

You don't need to try to bury them deep down or pretend they're not there. You don't have to apologize for them. It's totally okay that they are there; it doesn't make you *less* – it actually makes you like every single person on earth.

We all have insecurities. You might feel alone in yours, like everyone else seems to have it worked out. But nope – you are totally, completely, fully whole and worthy as you are, insecurities and all.

You don't need to push them away or scramble to fix them so they don't keep ruining your life. Newsflash – your insecurities won't ruin anything. They are there for you to acknowledge, give love to, support, hold gently, learn from, and eventually grow through.

The insecurities are often the places where you can experience the most enriching growth of all, because they contain the potential for you to step into new ways of being. They are where the gold is.

The parts of you that you wish were different, the things you wish you could change – those are just as much a part of you as anything else. They don't make you less. They don't make you weak. They make you *human*. And they put you in this perfect position of developing empathy for others.

They help you to connect to and relate to others in this shared humanity of having insecurities. What a great gift you can give to others... Accepting your insecurities is a bold move that can inspire others.

We all have them, those little voices in our heads that tell us we're not enough, that we're not worthy, that we don't measure up.

You don't have to feel scared of these insecurities, or feel like they will take over and sabotage your life. They won't. Especially when you welcome them, and *work with them*, not **against them**. They have more power over you when you deny their existence and try to fight them.

It's okay to have doubts about yourself. Your doubts doesn't define you. They're just feelings, and feelings don't have to control your worth.

Your insecurities don't make you unlovable, unworthy, or incapable. They don't take away from your beauty or your value or your strengths. They are just part of being a growing, evolving human.

Every time you feel insecure, you have the opportunity to show yourself kindness. Every time you acknowledge your insecurities, you can choose to embrace them, accept them, and let them teach you something new about life.

Your insecurities don't need to be fixed. They don't need to be erased. They are welcome, just like every other part of you.

You are whole, even in your imperfection. You are worthy, even in your doubt. And you are enough, with all of your insecurities.

You Are Loved,
Just As You Are

Stop for a second. Let this sink in: *You are loved*, just as you are.

No need to be something to earn love. No need to reach some ideal of perfection to be worthy of love. No need to change yourself for anyone else. You are not meant to prove you're worthy of love.

Love doesn't ask for proof. Love doesn't require certain conditions in order to flow through you. Love doesn't want you to bend over backward being someone you're not. Love wants to love you exactly the way you are.

Proving yourself in order to be loved isn't how you get the fulfilling kind of love you really want. That's not how love works. Even if we have believed this for a long time. Of course, you might have learned that. It's a normal thing to learn as children that love should be earned. But that doesn't mean it is true.

You can let go of that story now.

You are simply meant to be open to the love that life wants to give you. And life has so much love it wants to give you, even if it doesn't feel like it right now. The love you're looking for starts within you. You are deserving of love in all forms, no strings attached. You don't have to do anything to be worthy of it.

You don't have to give more than you've already given. You don't have to keep showing the world how valuable you are so that it will finally see that you can be loved. Life already knows that you are lovable simply because you exist.

Can you try to really let this sink in? You are loved just as you are, with all your imperfections, as well as the things that make you feel proud about yourself.

Loving yourself as you are doesn't mean you won't keep growing and shifting and reaching more healthy ways of being.

Loving who you are now doesn't mean that the parts that you'd like to continue to heal will stay the same and not change. Loving who you are doesn't stop growth, it actually helps you to grow in a more peaceful and graceful way.

I know, sometimes it feels like love is something you have to chase. Maybe you've felt unworthy or unloved in the past.

Maybe you've thought that love comes with conditions or that you need to be perfect to receive it.

Maybe the relationships you had gave you strong proof of these stories. But it doesn't mean that these stories are or were ever true.

True love, real love, doesn't come with strings. It doesn't require a checklist of things you have to do. Love is simply there, ready to embrace you exactly as you are. All of you. Right now.

Truly, right now, it's there.

Maybe you can even touch it as you read these words. Reach within and see if you can feel even a small slither of the love that is patiently waiting there for you to connect with. Even if you can't feel it, know that it is there. You will feel it.

You are loved. Just as you are. You are lovable, even in your mess. You are worthy of the greatest love life has to give you. Right. Now.

You Deserve To Have Your Boundaries Accepted

Your boundaries are non-negotiable. They're not something to be minimized or ignored just to make others feel more comfortable. They are not up for discussion because others aren't happy that you have those boundaries.

Your boundaries deserve to be accepted without question. They deserve to be honored without explanation. You are allowed to create the space you need. You are allowed to say "no" without guilt. And you are certainly allowed and to protect your peace at all costs.

What you need in life matters. What you need from others matters. And you deserve to have that respected.

Your boundaries might be argued with. Some people may even take your boundaries as a personal attack towards them. Whatever stories and judgments they have about your boundaries, remember that you shouldn't ever have to compromise them just to make someone else "feel better." Anyone who is not able to accept your boundaries is not someone to keep in your life.

It's easy to feel like you're being unreasonable when you put your foot down and someone doesn't like it. It is understandable that you feel guilty when you set a boundary that doesn't line up with someone else's agenda.

But the truth is you are not unreasonable. Your needs are valid. Your comfort is important. You are not here to bend over backwards to make others feel better at the expense of your own well-being.

That is not healthy, and it is not what you are worth. You are worth having your boundaries accepted and valued, no matter what. Even if someone doesn't have the same boundaries. Even if their no isn't the same as your no. That doesn't matter. What matters is that you are listened to.

It's not selfish to take care of yourself. It's necessary. You don't have to feel bad for needing time alone. You don't have to apologize for saying no. You don't need to justify your choices or give a lengthy explanation for why you can't or won't do something. Your boundaries are yours, and they don't need to make sense to anyone else. What matters is that they make sense to you.

Own your boundaries. Know that you are the only one who can protect them. And if that means walking away from people or situations that do not respect your boundaries, then do that. That is how you protect yourself.

If someone can't accept your boundaries, that's on them, not you. It's not your job to make everyone else comfortable with your needs. You are not here to be the one who always accommodates, always gives in, and always sacrifices. You're here to live your life in a way that feels right for *you*. And that's exactly what you deserve.

You deserve to have your limits honored. And you deserve to say "enough" when enough is enough. Your boundaries are not a reflection of you being difficult – they're a reflection of you knowing your worth. You are worthy of love, care, and space to breathe. And anyone who truly values you will respect your boundaries.

It's Okay To
Ask For Help

So, you think you need to handle everything on your own?

You don't want to burden anyone else with your stuff. You'd rather not make anyone else obligated to help you. You don't want people to think that you're a nuisance.

But there's something you're missing here...

It's not only okay to ask for help; **people want to help.** You don't have to carry the everything all by yourself. You don't have to struggle alone. And people don't want that for you either.

Whether they know you or not, there are so many people who are ready and willing to lend a helping hand. They can be family, a good friend, an acquaintance, or quite often, a stranger.

When you don't ask for help, you're robbing others of the gratifying feeling they get from helping you. You might think it is taking them off the hook, but actually, it is only distancing yourself from them.

There's strength in asking for support.

Your receptivity is a superpower.

It doesn't make you weak to ask for help; it makes you wise. And it doesn't make people see you as weak. It makes people admire your courage to admit that you aren't indestructible. This is a gift for others, as they start to realize that they are also allowed to ask for help. They, too, don't have to do it all alone.

You don't need to do it all. When you ask for help, you give others the chance to be there for you. They want to support you. They want to show up for you. Just like how you want to show up for others. That good feeling you get when you help others?That's a feeling you can also allow others to access when you allow them to help you. There's a warmth that you exude when you ask for help.

We're all in this together, and we don't have to go through it alone.

It's so much more fulfilling when we aren't alone. It's a lovely feeling to be helped when you allow it. When you have company, especially in the hard times, is a soothing balm to your soul.

Whether it's a simple favor or a deeper, more meaningful task, asking for help will connect you more deeply to others, soften your hardness around having to bear the burden alone. It's time to give others a chance to show up and feel good by supporting you.

No one expects you to have all the answers. No one actually wants you to struggle alone. Maybe today is the day you ask for what you need. It's okay. You don't have to do it all alone.

You Are
Allowed To
Rest

Rest is not something that you need to earn. You don't have to work yourself to the bone before you're "allowed" to rest.

Rest is just as important as everything else.

Actually, you already know how hard it is to try to do all the things when you haven't rested properly.

Rest is essential.

But of course, you probably have a million things on your mind, and taking a break might feel like a luxury you can't afford. Instead of focusing on how deserving you are of it, read these words: ***rest doesn't need a reason.***

How does that feel in your body when you hear this?

It's okay if you don't fully believe it. It's okay if you still feel attached to the idea that rest needs to be earned. That doesn't mean that you can't experiment with resting.

How about you give it a go?

Maybe today, you can try giving yourself permission to rest. Just to see how it feels. You don't have to be doing something all the time to feel like you matter. It's okay to stop, take a breath, and just... Be. Imagine just sitting, doing nothing, without feeling guilty. You're allowed to experience that. It really is possible.

I know you want to show up 120% for the people you care about, for your mission, for yourself... But without rest, how can you truly show up with the energy that you want to give? It is through the very act of resting that you fill yourself up again to be able to give your all.

You can do that again, but first, rest. Rest is what will help get you back there again.

You've been through a lot. You've done a lot (even if your mind tells you it's not enough), and it's okay to step back for a second, pause, and do absolutely nothing productive or "important" except the very important task of resting.

You don't need to explain it to anyone. You deserve it. Go rest. And don't forget to enjoy it.

You Can Trust Yourself

It feels nice when other people validate us. But you know what feels better?

Trusting yourself.

Honestly. It feels so much better than needing to have someone else approve your ideas, feelings, and decisions all of the time.

Of course, it feels good when people can give us that, and it's beautiful to receive, for sure. But when you realize that you can actually give yourself this nice feeling, too, it's a game changer. It means that you don't need to rely on others to feel validated.

Seek advice and support whenever you desire – it doesn't mean that you don't get to enjoy that anymore.

But know that you are worthy of your own trust. You can trust in your decisions, your ideas, and your feelings.

And sometimes, others won't be able to trust in those things, so all we have left is ourselves.

To trust yourself in the face of others doubting you, THAT feels good. You will start to realize that you are your own best friend. You are your biggest supporter. You are the one who holds the key to the validation that feels so good to receive at any moment.

If people are doubting you right now, that's okay. Let them. They don't know what you know. They can't feel what you feel. And ultimately, they're not living your life. You are.

You have everything you need inside of you. You have the answers. You have the strength. You have the wisdom. You already know what is right, even if you doubt it.

You've always known what's best for you. Your instincts have carried you this far, and they'll continue to guide you. Your instincts actually lead you to the people who will offer that extra support and helpful advice, too. But, first and foremost, you are your best advice-giver.

It's okay to make mistakes. It's okay to not have all the answers right away. That doesn't mean you can't trust yourself. That's how you learn and refine and build more wisdom.

You've survived everything you've been through so far. You've even thrived through things you probably never thought you could.

You can trust yourself to figure it out. You are stronger than you realize, and you are more capable than you give yourself credit for. You don't need anyone else to tell you what to do.

You really don't. And you also don't need to push others' feedback away, either. It's not one or the other.

Receive feedback, insight, and reflections, and then allow yourself to trust that you will resonate with what is true for you. Let yourself receive support, and make sure that you are also receiving your own support. You can trust yourself.

It's okay if you still feel that you can't yet. That's normal. But know that you truly don't need anyone else's tick of approval before you make a decision, or honor your feelings, or say no to something. Let them support. Let them hold you. And remember that you can still trust yourself.

Trust is built, day by day, through small moments. Notice all of the ways that you showed up for yourself today; all of the ways you cared for yourself already (even if it was just drinking a sip of water – you gave yourself that, you are showing up for yourself).

You can trust in yourself. And more and more, you will.

Your Feelings
Are Valid

Whatever you're feeling right now. *It's valid.*

Happy, sad, confused, or angry? Flat? Bored? Uninspired? Insecure? Your feelings matter. All of them. Every single one of them. Yes, even the feelings you don't want to be feeling. They're valid, too. You don't need anyone's permission to feel what you're feeling.

If you're trying to hide your emotions or push them down, thinking they're not "good" enough to feel, or not important, or that they're "bad" feelings, or that you're overreacting, just pause for a moment and remember this, *your feelings are real.*

You don't even have a reason for feeling what you feel. Can you let yourself feel whatever is there without having to make sense of it?

You don't have to apologize for how you feel right now, even if it seems trivial. It's not trivial. That feeling is there. That is your reality. And that's 1 billion percent okay.

Feelings can be frustrating, they can feel exhausting, and even scare us sometimes. It's easy to wonder whether you're actually safe enough to feel something so uncomfortable. But remember this: throughout your life, there have been many feelings that seemed like they would never end, but they always did. They always changed.

That will eventually happen, too. But you don't even have to think about that right now.

Let them be there.

Let yourself feel what you feel. It doesn't mean you have to work out why or even believe in the feeling. Whether the feeling contains wisdom, something insightful to show you, or is just coming from a wounded response or reaction; regardless of the reason, let it be there.

It's okay to feel angry when things aren't fair. Of course, you feel sad when you're disappointed. It's okay to feel overwhelmed when life feels like it's too much. It's okay to feel hurt. It's okay to not have a clue what you're feeling. You don't need to justify your feelings to anyone, *not even yourself.* You won't have to carry this feeling forever. But right now isn't even the time to think about it.

Just let yourself feel. You are safe to feel.

Let The Guilt Go

Whatever you did. Whatever you said. Whatever it caused.

Let the guilt go.

Guilt serves no one – not you and not anyone else. It's a heavy burden that doesn't make you a better person. It just holds you back from moving forward because of the energy it is draining from you.

You don't need to carry that around anymore.

You don't need to feel guilty for what you did, for taking care of yourself, for saying no, or for making your mistakes. There's no rule that says you have to feel guilty to make it right again.

And yes, maybe others might try to push guilt onto you. They've also learned that guilt might somehow fix things (p.s. it doesn't), so these people often try to do that to others, too. That doesn't mean it leads to a solution. And you don't have to accept the guilt that they're trying to pass onto you. Say a loving, silent, *no thank you* to that.

What does lead to the resolution you're looking for? Making changes through making amends and moving forward by looking forward. Guilt actually just stifles that process because you're looking behind you and letting it consume your vision.

It's up to you whether you take hold of the guilt others are trying to pass on to you.

It's up to you whether you believe it or hold it as your own.

It's within your power to let go of the guilt.

You've made mistakes. Maybe you showed up in a way that you don't feel great about. Maybe you really hurt someone. Can you acknowledge that without trying to punish yourself? Can you sit with the truth of it, let it humble you, and then, let it rest?

You don't need to keep carrying guilt as some kind of self-punishment. You truly don't. Thank the part of you that is trying to do that out of a misguided idea that it'll make you a better person, somehow. It won't, but part of you has believed that it will. You learned that a long time ago. It's okay that this is how you've been operating. It's okay that you've been treating yourself this way.

Now, it is time to break this pattern. You don't need to accept harsh treatment of yourself anymore. You never deserved that.

Letting go of guilt doesn't mean you don't care. It doesn't mean that you don't have remorse. It doesn't mean that you won't do better, next time.

Letting go of guilt means you're choosing peace. It means you're choosing forgiveness. It means releasing the heaviness so you can keep moving forward, learning from your past, and showing up how you desire to be.

It will free you, and actually give you the outcome that the guilt is sneakily trying to create (some sort of resolution and peace).

That is the true irony of it; that by letting go of the guilt, you actually land to the place that the guilt was always trying to get you – *to make things right again.*

When you let it go, you're in a better place to show up for those around you. You can't give from an empty cup. You can't make yourself feel bad, and then expect yourself to make others feel good from that place. Guilt is stopping you from moving forward, learning, forgiving, loving, and ultimately, creating a peaceful outcome.

So, let it go. You deserve to let it go. No matter what happened. You deserve to let the guilt go.

You Don't Need To Have All The Answers Right Now

It's okay to not know exactly where you're going. It's okay to not have a step-by-step plan laid out. You really don't need to have every single thing figured out.

No idea what the solution is? That's okay.

If you truly don't know how to move through something and what the answers are, it's okay. You are allowed to not know. Nothing terrible will happen if you don't have all of the answers right now.

The world might try to make you feel like you should know exactly what you're doing, when, how and every other little detail, as if you should have it all together. But that's not how life works.

Life doesn't come with a set of instructions that we follow step-by-step. Many answers uncover themselves slowly, and some answers come fast.

Sometimes, you'll have the solution, and other times, someone else will offer that clarity. To expect yourself to have all of the answers is putting a lot of unnecessary pressure on yourself.

You're allowed to feel uncertain, you're allowed to ask questions, and you're allowed to take time to find your way to the answers. You don't need to have those answers yesterday. And maybe you won't have them tomorrow. You don't need to know how they will come. Forcing an answer isn't what you deserve. You don't need to push and rush to fine answers.

They will come when they're meant to. Sometimes, the most meaningful parts of your journey are the moments where you're sitting in the question. Those times where you are without any idea of what will happen and how to move forward.

This is where magic has the potential to happen. When you haven't yet decided how it is going to be, you are open to how it might be (especially different from anything you could have thought up yourself).

There's no deadline on figuring things out. As you grow, your understanding deepens, and what once seemed unclear will start to make sense. But it isn't going to happen on anyone else's timeline, or your own made up timeline.

It'll happen in the time it happens. It might not sound great to hear all of this right now, if you're feeling very stuck in the mindset that you need to have the answers right now. It's okay that you just want to know.

You don't need to shame that part of yourself and make it wrong just because you're understanding that all answers aren't always going to come instantly. Maybe you can accept that you want clarity faster, and still find peace in not knowing, at the same time.

You don't need the answers today. You don't need them right now. You're exactly where you need to be, learning what you need to learn. You're allowed to be in the mess, to be in the unknown, because that's where growth lives. That is where magic can unfold.

You don't have to have all the answers right now. You're doing just fine. Keep being in the question. Maybe soon, you might even enjoy not knowing just yet.

You Deserve
Joy

Do you feel like you have to earn joy? That before you feel happy, you need to achieve something first? That in order to let yourself feel positive and great, you need to check every single box off your to-do list?

There is no need to wait for the right time to feel joy, or to prove you're worthy of happiness. *Joy is yours, right here, right now.* Without you needing to accomplish anything first to feel it.

You deserve to be happy, and you deserve to move away from what doesn't make you feel happy.

You deserve to be with people who bring out the sunshine in your life. You deserve to have people support your joy and actively seek to make you feel good. You deserve to care about your state of joy and to prioritize it. It's not trivial at all. It is important, and your joy deserves your attention.

You deserve to put energy into the things that create joy in your life. You deserve to design your life to have many more moments of joy. You deserve to want a life that isn't so dark, heavy, or hard.

I know it's easy to believe that life should be hard and joy should be a reward only. The world tells us so. And you've probably even told yourself this, too.

But if you were to ask yourself now if you really wanted to live this way, what would your answer be?

Do you really want to make your happiness an afterthought, and just wait for it to come along, hoping that eventually it'll be there?

Don't wait for everything to fall into place before you allow yourself to feel good.

The small, everyday moments are where joy lives. It's the quiet, peaceful times where you sit reading a good book. Or in a random, casual conversation with someone. It's being completely lost in fits of laughter with a friend, seeing a ridiculous meme, the smell of freshly washed sheets, a stranger being kind to you, the sound of rain tapping on your roof, the first bite of a great apple, or the warmth of the sun on your skin.

Joy isn't always a grand event (although those are great). And it's true that joy does come when we achieve big things, but that's not the only way we can feel joy. Joy is a patient invitation, just waiting for you to say yes so it can flood right through you.

It's right here, sitting next to you, waiting for you to accept it.

And remember, it's okay to feel happy even when things aren't perfect. It's okay to feel happy even when others aren't happy. You deserve to embrace the small moments and soak up happiness in them. Your joy isn't a reward for anything at all. It is a feeling that can be created at any moment.

It's here, now, ready to be welcomed. You deserve to welcome joy *today*.

You Are Not Alone

If you feel isolated, separated, different, alone in your struggles. Read these words...

You are not alone.

It's understandable if you don't fully believe that. It's easy to believe that no one else understands what you really feel or that you're walking through life without anyone to share it with.

Maybe it is true that you haven't spent much time with others or haven't felt understood as you are. But even so, remember this: There are others who care about you. Even if you haven't met them yet.

There are so many people who not only have the capacity, time, energy, and willingness to listen, understand, and support you but who also have been through what you're going through right now.

You don't need to face everything on your own. You can ask for support. You can seek out company purely because you want to feel less alone.

And even when you are there, without anyone else by your side, know that you aren't ever really alone. If you still feel that way, it's okay. You won't always feel this lonely.

Even if you don't always feel like it, there's always support out there. Sometimes, it's about reaching out. Sometimes, it is about accepting that you feel alone, and not shaming yourself for feeling this way.

Other times, it's just knowing that you are surrounded by love—even if you can't see it in that moment.

You're part of this shared experience of life. You matter. You are seen. Can you feel seen by the sky? By the trees? By the stranger walking past you with a small smile? By the people who have been there for you at some point in your life? By an unseen energy that surrounds you? Maybe that's God, the universe, or something else that you connect with.

Sure, someone else can never truly understand the unique experience that it is to be inside of yourself. We have a hard time understanding ourselves as we are, too. But that doesn't mean you're alone.

We can share the company of others, and know that it's okay if they don't fully relate to us. It doesn't mean we have to suffer in alone-ness. It means we're unique and have a special connection only we can have with ourselves.

Not being with any other person right now also doesn't mean you have to be alone. You are with you.

Your 5-year-old self exists within you. Your 12-year-old self. Every version of you that has ever been is there within you. So, too, is your wise self; that part of you that can observe yourself, that part of you that has greater awareness and perception of what you feel. Even the potential versions of you that aren't yet here. They are with you. The you reading this right now is also with you.

You are not alone. You are connected, and you don't have to even know what it is you're connected to.

Just know, you're never really alone.

You're Not Too Much

Think you're too much, huh?

Too bold, loud, bright, weird, big, opinionated, energetic...

Maybe you are **a lot.** Maybe for some people you seem "too much" for them. But that doesn't mean you're **too much.** You're not too loud, too big, too emotional, too ambitious, too anything. If someone tells you that, they just don't gel with your energy.

They might not know how to handle your fire, your worldview, your quirks, and your uniqueness. That's not their fault or your fault. That's just non-alignment.

You are really not here to fit into some neat little box that the world has decided is "acceptable." You are not here to make people feel comfortable by dimming your light (by the way, it doesn't even work. Often, making yourself smaller doesn't actually create comfort for anyone).

You are allowed to take up space. You are allowed to show up fully – flaws, emotions, limitations, insecurities, power, and all. You don't have to shrink yourself just because it makes someone else feel better. You're not meant to be *easy* to handle and that's what makes you remarkable.

Think about it. All those times you've been told you're too much? What they really mean is that you're *more*. You're more than what they can see, more than they can comprehend. Your energy, your dreams, your intensity – those are your superpowers.

Don't let anyone make you believe that being *you* is too much. You are exactly what the world needs even if it's not always ready for you.

The moments where your emotions are too much? All that is happening there is that your emotions may not be something that is within their capacity to navigate. That's okay. It's not their fault. It's not your flaw.

People will either be able to show up or not. People will either be able to receive you or not. That is the simple truth of it. It's not a comment on your character that your energy might be too much for others to be able to navigate.

It's not a definitive judgment that you should be "less." It just means that you're still finding the people in your life who really resonate with you. That takes time and it will also change overtime.

The right people? They will love every bit of you, and have the capacity to show up for the loud parts, the quiet parts, the messy parts, the imperfect parts. They will want all of it and not feel overwhelmed by who you are. You don't have to wait for them to "approve."

You're not a project to be molded into someone else's idea of "acceptable." You are already enough just as you are.

It starts with you feeling and owning the truth of that. It starts with you accepting your enough-ness, and dropping the story of your too-much-ness.

You can stop apologizing now. You can stop holding back. You are not here to play small. You're here to *live* – big, bold, and unapologetic. You are everything you need to be. And that's exactly the right amount.

Maybe there's even more for you to be? Forget "too much", what about... "more please?"

Be Gentle With Yourself

The world is tough enough as it is.

You don't need to bring that toughness onto yourself, too.

Be gentle with yourself.

You don't have to pile on more pressure, more expectations, or more guilt. You've got enough going on already.

Even if it doesn't feel like it, you deserve a little kindness from yourself.

It's okay if you're not perfect. It's okay if you don't have everything figured out. It's okay if you've made mistakes; yes, even those huge "unforgivable" mistakes that you're still holding onto. You are still worthy of your own gentleness. Your tender, slow presence.

Treat yourself as you would a delicate baby kitten (or any other precious living thing that melts your heart). How would you speak to yourself if you were really approaching yourself with gentleness?

How would it feel to have someone be soft, kind, loving, and sweet to you (not because you earned it, but because you deserve it just as you are)...

Know this: You're doing your best. And that's enough. You don't need to have it all together all the time. Even when you look back and see that you didn't do "great," you still did the best that you could with your knowledge and capacity. Maybe your own hurt drove you to hurt others. Maybe your wounding ran the show and led you to act in ways you don't feel great about...

Does that really mean you should block yourself from being kind and gentle with yourself? No. Definitely not. Because it doesn't create anything good. It doesn't lead you to the peace you're looking for.

There's no medal for being hard on yourself, no reward for pushing yourself to the limit.

There's no beauty that comes from harsh, resistant energy. You won't get to happiness by making yourself suffer. You won't get to peace by not being kind to yourself. So, give yourself permission to rest. To soften. Give yourself grace. You're not behind. You're not failing. You're not bad. You're not wrong. You're not unworthy. You deserve love, especially from yourself.

You're allowed to slow down. You're allowed to be gentle. Take a deep breath and a long, slow exhalation, breathing out all of the harsh, hard energy that you really don't need anymore.

Feel that softening?

That's yours. That is kindness and gentleness in action. That is what will bring with it peace, beauty, and ease. It's actually not so difficult or complex to do. You can. Right now. Give yourself that.

You Are Doing Your Best

Hey. Tough love time.

Stop talking down to yourself. Stop with the *couldda, shouldda, woudda* energy. Stop with the recrimination and shaming of your mistakes and past actions.

You *are* doing your best. Even when you don't feel like it.

It's easy to get so caught up in what we haven't done yet, what we could have done better, or how far we think we have to go. And that leaves us feeling lack. Like we should know better, be better, do better, and stop failing so much.

That mentality doesn't just make you feel bad, but it'll actually prevent you from showing up how you want to.

It'll stop you from growing, expanding, and reaching those goals.

Because no goal will be reached happily by forcing your way through it as you tell yourself negative stories about yourself. You might reach the finish line, but it'll feel empty and without any real satisfaction because you spent the whole journey feeling like you were lacking. Which means when you get there, you'll continue to feel that lack.

The secret to feeling good? Feel good.

Okay, that sounds silly, but it's true. If you don't feel good on your journey to the goal of feeling good, you won't miraculously feel good at the end of the journey.

You want to feel better? It won't happen by making yourself feel bad for not doing and being *better*.

And a second tip – don't get caught in the trap of making yourself feel bad for feeling bad. If you have been hard on yourself, then forgive yourself for that and start inviting softness in. Feeling bad about feeling bad only gets you to feel worse...

Know that you're doing your best, right now. Even when you've been hard with yourself, you've been doing the best you can. No need to be harder on yourself.

That doesn't mean that there's no room to grow and that there won't be an *even better* later. Acknowledging that you're doing your best now is what frees you from putting pressure, heaviness, and lack onto yourself, making you feel that you should be different.

Being different will happen naturally. Growth will happen. You will move forward, if you let yourself. Being harsh with yourself will only make that process of growth more difficult.

With that new lightness of self forgiveness, you can keep moving forward without so much weight to carry. You don't need to be perfect. You don't need to be at the finish line already. What matters is that you're trying.

When you take a step back and look at all you've been through, all you've accomplished, you realize that you've actually been doing great. Even in your mistakes, the fact that you can look back and learn from them means that you're doing great. The fact that you are simply trying, means you are doing great. And trying might simply look like staying in bed all day. Sometimes that's the best you can do; and that's okay. Give yourself a pat on the back.

Seriously.

I won't keep writing until you do.

....

I hope you did. Because you deserve to recognize that you're doing your best. No more critical thoughts and stories about yourself needed. You'll keep evolving and doing better. Trust that. Be kind to yourself, and let that kindness boost your growth.

Remember that there is no failure in trying and not reaching the standards you thought you would. You tried and that is so beautiful. You showed up. Whatever that meant. There's a lot of growth in trying.

You are growing, even when it doesn't feel like it. You are doing enough, even if it doesn't seem like it. You're doing the best you can with what you have, what you know, and how you feel. And that deserves to be acknowledged.

You Are
Stronger Than
You Think

Excuse me.

Do you really think you're weak? Do you really believe
that you don't have a power within you that can with-
stand any storm? Do you really feel that you won't be able
to make it through?

You are stronger than you think. You've been through so
much. And yet, here you are. Maybe you feel battered and
bruised right now, maybe you don't feel the strength, but
that doesn't mean that you aren't strong.

Sometimes, strength feels like we can do absolutely anything. Sometimes, strength feels like barely holding on.
Sometimes, strength feels like we are ready for whatever comes our way. Sometimes, strength feels like we're
clinging onto the cliff edge by a single slipping finger.

Even on the days when you feel like you're falling apart, your strength is in existing. It's easy to forget how powerful you are. You've survived tough times, and you've come out the other side.

You might not believe it right now, especially if you don't feel like you're thriving, but you've gained wisdom and insight, and so many more gifts from what you've gone through.

You don't need to see it right now, but you are a force. You've got this. Whatever comes next, you are more than capable of handling it. You are stronger than you think.

Keep going. Whether that's sprinting and bounding over obstacles or crawling on the ground inch by inch, your strength is there.

The power is there. It's yours. Claim it. Know it. Feel it. It's time to believe it.

You will start to see it, more and more. You will feel it, more and more. And it will inspire you to keep moving. One day, it'll be more than just surviving. You'll realize that your strength is inviting you to thrive. And thrive, you will.

It's Okay To Take Your Time

The world tells you to rush.

To do more, to be faster. To keep up with the pace of everyone around you. To hustle and then hustle harder.

That voice seems so normal that we begin to believe it. We tell ourselves the same things; to do more, be more, accomplish more, take on more, and only rest once it has been earned.

Cut out all the noise for a moment. Pause. Take a breath. And know that it's 100 million percent okay to take your time. Whether it's going at a snails pace or pausing entirely.

You don't have to make decisions on someone else's timeline. You don't have to accomplish all the things right now. You don't have to put that pressure on yourself. You don't need to reply instantly, complete the tasks straight away, and rush through the piling list of things, just to get to the next pile of things. You don't have to figure it all out right now.

Life is not a race. And there's no medal at the end for the fastest.

And you have the right to move at your own pace. Sometimes, the most important (and even productive) thing you can do is to slow down. But you don't have to slow down purely because it will fuel productivity.

You deserve to slow down. Period. No reason. No explanation needed; not for yourself or anyone else. Take a moment to breathe, to pause, to rest, to reflect, to really think things through. There's no need to rush. Even if someone else is expecting you, too.

Let them. It's only because that's how they are treating themselves. But you don't need to buy into this story anymore. You don't need to place that expectation on yourself either. You have time to figure it out and to find your way, at your own pace.

You will get where you need to go, in your own time. Trust that. Lean back. Slow down. Ease up. **It's okay to take your time.**

There Is Hope

I know you want to give up. It's okay that you feel that way.

We've all felt that way. But, know that you can keep holding on to the hope, even if it's the tiniest light of hope. That's something to keep holding onto.

Hold onto that little light that is peaking through the dark clouds. I know it seems like that light will go out, and they will only be darkness left, but know that there is always hope.

No matter how futile it seems, there's hope. No matter how much you can't see ahead, know that beyond what you can see, there's hope. No matter how little progress you've made, or how unlikely it is to reach that vision; know that there is still always hope.

Life has a way of surprising us, so be open to being surprised. You don't have to fully believe it all right now.

You don't have to know what will happen. Just know that as long as you are here, breathing, existing; there is always hope.

Let that hope soften your heart. Let it release some of that fear. Let is soothe the anxiety.

There is hope.

Let that hope spark just a little bit of inspiration. Let the hope be there, and maybe it even starts to grow.

You Are Not Defined By Your Mistakes

Yes, you've made mistakes. Probably many. Some small and some huge. Some that didn't really have much of an impact on things, and some that have you still cleaning up the mess.

It doesn't matter how many mistakes you've made, or how big they were, and how many more mistakes you will make; they are *not you.*

You are not defined by your mistakes. They don't make you a failure. They don't make you a bad person. You are no less worthy of love and care and kindness. You don't have to earn back your value after making a mistake by punishing yourself.

Your mistakes are just that; mistakes. And you can always start again.

If you catch yourself thinking about the mistakes, and beating yourself up for them; stop, breathe, and let it go. They happened, and you are not the same person who made that mistake. Whether it was 10 years ago or 10 minutes ago, the knowledge and understanding you have now makes you a different person. And the very fact that you can see it was a mistake shows that you have grown already.

Guess what? You're going to make mistakes again. Yep. It's true. And you're still going to be worthy of kindness, care, love, and forgiveness.

You are growing, learning, and doing the best you can, and sometimes doing the best we can means making mistakes along the way.

That's okay. **Your mistakes don't define you.**

How you keep showing up, how you are able to let go, forgive, and find your peace again; that is what defines your character and it is what either makes your journey forward more smooth (or not).

You get to choose; to be defined by your mistakes, or to not be defined by them. That is your choice and totally within your power.

Relax, release, and know that it's okay that you have made mistakes. You're okay. You will be okay.

You're worthy of your forgiveness.

You Are Allowed To Let Go

You're not the only one who holds onto things - thoughts, feelings, memories, patterns, habits, people...

It's very normal. But not always helpful.

Are you holding onto anger? Someone you know you need to release, but don't know how? Something you feel complete with, but unsure if you're ready to let go?

You're human. Of course, you're trying to hold on.

It's okay that you're holding on. But now it's time to let go. Not because you're reading these words, telling you to let go, but because you deserve to let go. You are 100% allowed to let go of what isn't aligned anymore.

You are allowed to let go of friendships, relationships, beliefs, ways of being, that job, that version of yourself... anything and everything.

You are allowed to let go because you can allow yourself to let go. Let go of what doesn't make you feel valued, at peace, and empowered.

It might not be easy. It might hurt at first. But holding onto something that's not benefiting you isn't helping you move forward and actually get to a place of feeling good, valued, loved, respected, and confident.

Letting go allows you to make space for what really matters to you, for new opportunities, people, places, patterns, and for healing. That space is needed, and it is yours to take, once you let yourself let go.

Letting go is also something you can do slowly, gracefully, or instantly. It's not pushing away. It's like opening your palm and letting go of something you were holding onto – it's a release, actually. It requires less energy than holding on, in many ways. Can you see that? Can you see that once you let go of holding on, you get back so much more energy? You will get to feel relief, softness, peace...

You deserve to be free from what holds you back. You deserve to release what isn't yours any longer. *You're allowed to let go.*

You Don't Need Anyone's Approval

If you've felt like you've lived in the shadow of others' opinions, constantly making sure that they approve of your decisions, it's time to release that.

You don't actually need their approval. Even if right now it feels like that is what you need to take action. It's normal to want others to agree and validate you, and you are allowed to want that and receive that.

It's normal to have an idea, and first want someone else to approve of it before you accept it yourself. Or to get someone else's "go-ahead" for that decision you've been thinking about.

But here's the reality - they aren't living your life. They aren't you. And while you and your life may matter to them (perhaps a very great deal), it will still never match the amount that your own life matters to you - because it is your life.

At the end of the day, your decisions are your own. They are personal to you, and you are the greatest authority on your life.

Sometimes you'll need to ask others to help become clear, and to make sense of your decisions and feelings. That's more than okay - it's so necessary to get reflections from others sometimes.

Just make sure that you treat yourself as a wise council, too. There are many times when your body and mind are communicating with you, giving you signals, signs, and information to take action in a certain direction.

It might not make sense to others, but that's okay. You don't need it to make sense to them.

Trust yourself. Know that relying on every single person to validate you, how you're living, what you're thinking and feeling; it's exhausting, and ultimately, someone will disagree, because we are all different people and see life in different ways.

What matters is that you give yourself the approval you're seeking.

You get to say YES to you. You get to decide.

You can start today by saying these words, *"I approve of myself, my decisions, and my feelings. I don't need others to agree. I agree with me, and that is more than enough."*

It's Okay
To Feel
Disconnected

You know that feeling when everything around you is distant, like you're a little too far from the world to really touch it? Like you're standing just outside the crowd, hearing the laughter but not quite part of it? Yeah, that's okay that you feel that way.

Feel disconnected from life or people right now? It's normal to feel this. It doesn't mean you will always feel this way.

We can feel disconnected from people we usually feel connected to. We can feel disconnected from our goals, or our life in general. It's not a pleasant feeling, of course, but it doesn't have to scare you or make you feel like something is terribly wrong.

Maybe something is off, and you will find the clarity soon enough. Simply accepting that you feel disconnected is the first step. And not making it wrong or bad.

You don't always have to be in sync with everything or everyone. It doesn't mean you've failed or that something is not okay. The moments where you feel disconnected are often the places where the most growth happens, even if you don't see it in the moment. Hindsight is funny like that.

It's okay to be out of alignment sometimes. We're all just figuring it out, trying to find our way in a world that constantly moves and shifts. And since we're always moving and shifting too, feeling out of whack is inevitable.

When you feel disconnected, instead of trying to force yourself back into something that doesn't fit, or rush to "connect" to something even if it's not truly right for you, just give yourself a moment.

Pause. Step back. Sit with that discomfort. Let it be what it is, without rushing to fill the gap.

Being disconnected doesn't mean you're lost. It doesn't mean you're failing. It just means you're in a space of transition. It's a space to also start to look inside and see if you might be able to create some connection with yourself, even in a small way.

You are allowed to drift.

You are allowed to be in a season where things feel unclear, where connections feel thin, or where you're just not quite sure where you belong.

It more than okay to feel as you feel. Even when you're disconnected, you're still worthy, valuable, lovable, and whole.

It's Okay To Change Your Goals

You've set goals. You've made plans. Maybe you've invested time, energy and resources into those goals. You wanted those things. And that was real.

But life isn't a straight line.

Things change. People grow. Ideas evolve. Feelings shift. What you wanted yesterday isn't always the same as what you want today. That is totally okay. It is 100% normal.

You are allowed to adjust, realign, redirect, stop, pivot, pause... Just because you have set goals, doesn't mean you are obligated to reach them.

Dedication, integrity, commitment - they are important, of course, and sometimes along the way to our goals we lose motivation, feel tired, and just don't feel like continuing. But that's different from realizing that you actually aren't aligned with your past goals anymore.

It's not "uncommitted' to change your goals. If you are truly committed to yourself and living a life that you are consciously creating, then changing your goals will be part of that.

Your goals aren't set in stone. They are flexible. They're changeable. Changing your goals means you're adapting and learning what works best for you.

It means you're honoring the fact that you evolve and change, and that who you are isn't a statue that will be frozen in time. That is a powerful thing to be present to, because you're opening yourself to the possibility that life can offer...

Things you haven't yet thought of. Plans you are yet to make.

Goals you're yet to discover. It's not only okay to change your goals, it's a sure thing that somewhere along the way your journey in life, you will change them.

You're doing great.

You Are Not Responsible For Others' Happiness

We've all been there, trying to make others happy, trying to fix their problems, trying to take on more than our fair share of the emotional load.

You've bent over backward to please them.

You've held your tongue and not said what was really on your mind and heart because you didn't want to hurt, disappoint, or rock the boat...

You've compromised on what you really wanted so that they can be happy. And where has this left you? Exhausted, sad, unheard, misunderstood, lonely, and not happy.

Why did we think that being responsible for others' happiness would magically make us happy, too? Sure, it's nice to make someone happy, but it's not our job; it's something we get to enjoy. It's a bonus. And it should always come from a place of fullness and alignment.

If making someone else happy means making yourself unhappy, then that equation doesn't add up. Eventually, you'll burn out. It's easy to believe that if we just do more for others, make them feel better, or sacrifice our own well-being we can fix things.

But it's not your job to fix them. You can't carry someone else's emotions for them. You can't solve their problems. You can support, love, and help, but you aren't responsible for taking on their stuff to the detriment of your own.

You are only responsible for your own feelings, your own actions, and your own happiness.

You can stop trying to be everything for everyone now. Let it go.

You're allowed to set boundaries and to say no when it's not your responsibility. You're allowed to ask for what you need, even if that might not totally make someone super thrilled. You're allowed to share your dreams and desires, for your own happiness.

You don't have to bear the weight of other people's happiness and scramble to micro-manage their emotions.

You are enough, just as you are. You don't need to make them happy for you to be worthy. You are worthy and enough now, without having to give and give all of the time.

They'll work it out. And when you step aside, you're giving them the gift of learning how to make themselves happy.

You're not extracting your care for them by letting go of this responsibility. Instead, you are caring for both of you by letting go of the reins.

So, let go.

Get yourself happy. And you'll start to see that others naturally become happier in your presence. It's funny how much happier people can get when you give them space to get happy on their own... And how much happier you get when you turn that energy to yourself.

Start with yourself.

You're responsible for your happiness. So, right now, choose to do something for the next few minutes, that you know will make you happy. Drop every other urgent thing. Don't read any more chapters until you give yourself that. And just have that little practice of giving it to yourself, first.

You deserve it.

You Are More Than Your To-Do List

Do you define yourself by what you get done?

Feel lime your worth is dependent on all the tasks you tick off the list?

We're all conditioned to believe that the more we check off our to-do list, the more valuable we are. There's a gratification we get from checking those things off, for sure. It's nice to make progress. It feels good to know that we are meeting goals, moving forward, and accomplishing things.

But whether you check the to-do list off or not really isn't the deciding factor of your worthiness. You don't become more worthy with every tick.

Does it feel that way? That's okay. You're not alone feeling like this. But it's important to remind yourself that you are not defined by how much you accomplish. You're not a machine designed to produce.

Your worth isn't tied to your productivity. It's tied to your humanity. Your are valuable and worthy simply because you exist. Full Stop. No arguments.

Let the noise of the world happen around you, let the world tell you to do and be more, but don't listen to it. You get to choose what story you are going to believe. You get to choose where you define your worthiness.

No one else but you.

You are worth letting go of the constant pressure to be busy. You can absolutely let go of the idea that being "productive" is the same as being valuable. You deserve to take breaks, to rest, to pause, to stop, to roll around on the floor all day and accomplish nothing.

Yes, even when you are a puddle of goo, feeling moody, flat, and haven't done anything at all that would be labeled as "productive", you are worthy. You are more than enough, without having to prove it.

There is nothing to prove. Your worth is already there. So, lay on the floor and be the goo, or get up and do the things - either way, your value has never left you.

It's Okay To
Say No

Even when it feels weird or wrong to say NO – sometimes it is absolutely the right thing to do. When you say YES to things that don't actually feel like a true YES, what you're doing is really saying NO to your happiness, peace, balance, values, and health.

You don't want to disappoint others, of course. You want to be liked and you want to be supportive. You want to be seen as someone who is reliable.

Your NO doesn't mean that you'll automatically lose friendships, connection, and respect. Actually, people respect you when you respect yourself more. Not everyone will like it, but you will get respect. And most of all, self respect.

If you have lost something by saying NO to something that really is a NO, then that was exactly what needed to exit your life (even if it hurts). That relationship needed to end. That job, that situation, that was right to end if your NO ended it.

Your NO is as valuable as your yes.

Your NO protects yourself from overworking, stress, and depletion.

Your NO respects yourself.

Your NO respects others by you not over-giving and compromising yourself. You don't respect another person when you compromise yourself.

Your NO is self-care.

Your NO is not selfish. Your NO might disappoint others, and that's okay. Your NO is your healthy boundary being expressed.

It's okay to prioritize yourself. It's essential to prioritize your health. And your NO does that.

Your NO is beautiful.

And sometimes it is harsh for others to hear. But you aren't responsible for their feelings. You're responsible for the integrity of yourself and how you show up. And that starts with knowing your YES and your NO.

Also, it's hard to trust a YES when it's the only option. A YES said out of obligation isn't really a true yes. When you say no, you're creating space for what truly matters.

You're allowing yourself to conserve your energy for the things that align with your goals, your values, and your well-being. And that well-being is the essential first step to be able to show up for others, and to be able to keep giving those true YESES.

You're allowed to stop saying YES when you really mean NO.

It's not only okay to say NO, it's a wonderful thing.

Just Existing
Is Enough

There is nothing you need to do to be enough.

Nowhere you have to be to be enough.

There are no accomplishments that'll make you more worthy of feeling full and content.

Your content isn't going to come with more success. Your enough-ness won't be found by reaching for all those things outside of you.

Getting that person won't make you enough. Neither will the money. Or the awards. The fame and popularity, they're not going to magically deliver you to the enough feeling that you are looking for.

You don't need to keep scrambling to find all the ways you can prove yourself.

You don't need a master plan. You don't need to fix, solve, or evolve any more. You will evolve, naturally, but not because it makes you more worthy to evolve. Simply because that's just how life works.

And you are part of the beautiful mess of life. The confusing wonderfulness of all of life's change, surprises, and difficulties. That is real, and you are part of that beauty, simply because you exist. You are an essential part of the tapestry of life, and you don't need to do anything more to earn your place here.

You have a place here. You are here. You are enough. You are worthy.

You can slow down now. Maybe even pause and rest. Melt. Soften. Let all the tension go.

Let yourself just exist. As you are. Just be, who you are. An ever-changing glorious spark of light in life.

You Are Already On The Right Path

If you're doubting yourself because things aren't happening as quickly as you want them to, or you're uncertain about the future, know this: *it's normal to feel that way.*

But that doesn't mean you aren't on the right path.

You're exactly where you need to be, even if it doesn't feel that way right now.

It's not only a new-age phrase that's often thrown around. It's true. But also, being told that we are in the right place right now can feel downright annoying when we feel fed up with life, the challenges, and the suffering we've been feeling.

But try this on for a moment; just because you can't see or yet feel that where you are is right, what about embracing that everything is, in fact, right, simply because you're here.

That's it.

It's right because that's where you are. How can it be wrong? The truth of life is that you are in this place right now, reading these words, in the phase of life you're in.

None of that is bad, wrong, too slow, or misaligned.

Every step you've taken, every decision you've made, has brought you to this point. What you're learning about life, yourself, what you want, what you don't want, how you wish to move forward, the goals you have... all of that has been put into your awareness and field because of the past steps you've taken. Even if they were mistakes, and things you wish you could change, do you truly wish you could change who you are right now.

Maybe you want to be more loving, soft, compassionate, clear, balanced, and that's okay. Everyone can always be more of those things - they aren't ever static goals that we just "achieve."

Just because you might not feel the things you want to feel yet, doesn't mean that you aren't in the right place now. And even that desire to grow and change is perfect. That desire is even more indication that you're on the right path.

There's no perfect path, and there's no best way to walk it. Even if it seems like others are walking the path more gracefully or fast than us (but I'll tell you now to stop comparing to anyone, especially curated online versions of people).

You might not have all the answers yet, but that's okay. This journey is about learning, growing, and trusting the process. You don't need to know everything right now.

Just keep moving forward. Keep trusting where you lead yourself. Keep moving at your own pace - sometimes that'll be fast, sometimes slow, sometimes it'll feel like you're not moving at all. It's all part of the journey, and it will continue to give you so many deep lessons, insight, inspiration, joy, peace, love, and everything in between.

Life will surprise you. Life will sometimes feel flat. You might feel impatient. All of these things are not bad or wrong or any indication that you're going off track.

Because here is the most important secret of all; there is no wrong or right path. Not really. Just your path.

That's it. This is your story. Your path. Your journey. And you're walking it wonderfully.

It's Okay To Ask For What You Need

You can ask for what you need.

Your needs are important. No matter how silly they might sound and feel. Your needs deserve to be heard and honored.

It's totally okay to ask for what you need. You don't have to do everything by yourself, and you definitely don't have to pretend that you're okay when you're not.

Sometimes, it feels like you should just handle everything on your own. As if asking for help is some kind of weakness. But it's not. It's actually very brave to be real with what you need and let others have the chance to help.

People want to help. People want to feel needed. And they absolutely want to trust that you will share with them what you need.

We get so used to pushing through, thinking we'll be fine, that we forget we're allowed to take a step back, pause, and ask for help. We forget it's okay to ask for a little extra; you're not too much for wanting and needing more, or something different. Whether it's time to yourself, help with something, a certain way you wish to be supported or loved, an action, some words, or just someone to listen – *you're allowed to want that.*

It's not too much. You don't need to apologize for needing things. You don't have to be superhuman. You are a perfectly imperfect human with needs, and there are many times where you alone cannot meet all of those needs.

You don't have to be "strong" all the time. You don't have to carry everything alone. Asking for what you need is part of taking care of yourself. And when you take care of yourself, you're able to show up better for everyone else, too.

So, don't hold back asking for what you need. Don't feel bad for needing something. We all need things. You can't pour from an empty cup, so go ahead and ask for what fills you.

Maybe you know that in order to feel grounded, balanced, or even vibrant and thriving, you need a certain something that isn't here right now. The only way you would ever receive that is by asking, not assuming people know what you need and then feeling sad that they aren't met.

You deserve to get what you need. Your needs are important. They are valid. They are wonderful. And they deserve to be respected.

Respect your own needs. Let them be heard.

You Deserve To Heal At Your Own Pace

You think you already need to be healed right now?

Absolutely not.

Healing takes time, and there is no perfect pace for healing. Also, are we ever fully healed? Like, we get to a place where we brush our hands off and say "welp that's that, guess I've reached perfection in all aspects of life..."

Sure, we can heal from certain experiences and heal old patterns and wounds, but ultimately, since you will always have more life to experience, which brings more challenges, there will also be more to heal.

Healing is a constant state of being, and maybe by simply being with what is, and looking forward to the vision of more peace and love, we are naturally healing along the way.

Maybe there's a very specific part of you that you know you need to heal – that's beautiful that you can recognize this. Just remember that healing is not linear.

It doesn't happen overnight, and it doesn't happen in this straight line. We feel healed, and then we go deeper and uncover another layer. We feel clear, and then something happens and triggers a part of us that is asking to be attended to.

You **can and will** heal this, if you have this strong intention, but it doesn't mean you have to be there already. Of course, you want to be there already, but trying to rush the process will not actually respect the pace that the healing really needs.

If you're recovering from something right now – you don't need to rush it. You are allowed to take all the time you need.

Don't let anyone else pressure you into feeling like you should be "over it" by now or that you should move faster. If you feel that pressure, give yourself the validation that you need.

Let yourself not compromise yourself, your pace, and your journey just because others have a different expectation.

Your healing is yours, and it doesn't follow anyone's timeline but your own.

You're doing the best you can. You are healing, already. You deserve to take the time you need.

You Are Allowed To Be A Work In Progress

You don't have to have it all figured out.

I know it might feel nice to finally have the solutions, answers, clarity, plans... Sure, that feels good. But it's not actually possible to have all the answers, because you'll keep having new questions. All the time.

You are moving, changing, and growing. Life is moving, changing, and evolving, so how could you ever have it all figured out? In a life where there is always new experiences, learning, and creation, it's not possible to have it all figured out in any one moment.

You're absolutely allowed to still be working on things; whether that's your physical or mental health, your habits, your goals... You're somewhere in the middle, not the end, and actually, you'll never reach the end anyway. You'll always be in the middle of something.

We can reach goals, but then they'll be another, and you'll be progressing towards that. You'll never NOT be in progress with something, so why not relax into the journey.

Relax into the progress. And let yourself just BE in that.

You're not alone in feeling like you should have your life sorted, have your career figured out, have a solid state of good mental health all of the time, or know exactly where you're going.

But the truth? You'll always still be figuring it out.

You'll reach one milestone, and another one will come. You'll find answers, and then more questions will arise. When you start to realize that you are always in progress anyway, you get to allow yourself to be that work in progress, and you'll find peace in that.

That peace and presence lets you actually enjoy the journey. Not just the journey to one goal, but the journey of life. *Every moment of every day.*

You're in the process. You get to make decisions, try new things, see what fits, and let go of what doesn't.

It's okay to take your time. There's no rush to get anywhere. If you're not exactly where you want to be yet, that's totally fine. You're still moving forward, even if it doesn't feel like it.

You don't need to have all the answers. You're allowed to make it up as you go along. It's enough, as it is. You're enough, as you are, right now.

Being in progress is just being. Go easy on yourself. Be where you are. Be the work in progress. Embrace the work in progress. Because this is life.

You Are Worthy Of Peaceful Relationships

You don't have to put up with connections that drain your energy. With relationships take more than they give you.

You deserve to have nourishing relationships. You get to have that. You don't need to compromise on your needs and desires.

You shouldn't ever be made to feel that you aren't worthy of peace and genuine care in your relationships. You shouldn't have to suffer through your connections.

Yes, human connection is hard sometimes, even with the most loving and healthy relationships. But you shouldn't have to struggle so hard, and feel so lost in your relationships. They are there to nourish you, not deplete you.

You're worthy of relationships that bring you calm, and that make you feel seen and understood, not overwhelmed.

You don't need to settle for negative and harmful energy or constant tension. Peace is not something you have to earn by enduring disrespect and chaos – it's something you deserve, for no other reason than that you exist. You're allowed to have relationships that lift you up, that make you feel comfortable, safe, and respected. You are absolutely allowed that.

It's okay to let go of relationships that don't bring you peace. You're not obligated to stick around just because you've been close with someone for a long time or because you feel like you should stay. If it doesn't feel right, if it doesn't bring you joy or support, it's okay to take a step back.

You are worthy of love that feels easy, of connections that feel warm and affirming, of spaces where you can just *be* without needing to constantly prove your worth.

You don't have to fight for respect, kindness, or peace. You deserve those things by simply being you.

You get to decide what's acceptable in your relationships and what isn't. You have every right to walk away from anything or anyone that disturbs your peace. And that's not selfish – that's self-care.

Don't settle for anything less than the peace and respect you deserve.

You are worthy of all the good, peaceful connections life has to offer.

You Don't Have To Keep Proving Yourself

What are you really trying to prove?

That you're lovable? You already are. It's a fact, no need to prove this to others. That you're worthy? Yep, you're already worthy as you are, without any need for someone else to approve of it.

You've already done enough, and you're enough just as you are. You don't have to keep showing people that you're worthy of love, respect, or success. You've got that, without needing to do more. You are worthy of all of it already. Done. Nothing to convince.

You don't need to earn your place every single day. You already belong. You don't have to keep trying to prove yourself, getting exhausted in the process.

It's okay to relax and just *be*. You can stop trying to convince everyone (including yourself) that you're enough. You already are. You don't need to hustle or overextend just to feel like you've earned your worth. There's nothing to earn.

You can't earn something that you already are inside. Imagine how it would feel to just stop for a second and think, "I don't need to prove anything right now."

Try that. Read those words, and let them sink in. Say those words a few times until you start to let yourself believe them. Release the pressure of proving. Let it go.

You've got everything you need to keep moving forward. Because *you* are who you need. Your own self-validation and love is all you need. No need to prove anything. Nothing to earn. Nothing to chase. Just keep being you, that's more than enough.

Give Your
Shame Love

Shame is one of those things we don't talk about enough, because it grows in the dark and by its very nature it wants to stay hidden.

It creeps in quietly, maybe from something you did, something you didn't do, or just that nagging feeling that maybe you're not enough. It sticks with you, makes you feel small with the stories the shame tells us, like the one where you have to hide parts of yourself away in order to be accepted, loved, safe, or simply worthy of existing.

You don't need to hide. You don't need to run from that feeling. You don't need to push anything away. All parts of you are welcome, even the shame for things you have done, said, didn't do, didn't say...

Shame doesn't go anywhere when you try to ignore it. And the stories you tell yourself about what you are ashamed of, they only go deeper.

Give your shame love, not as a way to justify or excuse what you no longer want in your life, and how you don't wish to continue to show up, but as a way to heal.

What you are ashamed of doesn't need more judgment. It needs gentleness. It needs compassion. It's okay to be where you are, feeling what you're feeling. That doesn't make you bad or less than.

Anything you've done is worthy of forgiveness and love.

You are worthy of forgiveness and love.

Shame gets even louder when we try to shut it down. But when we stop fighting it, we can finally give ourselves the permission to just *be*. And in that space of being with the shame that is hiding the parts of us that we don't like, we get to actually look at those parts of us not with disgust, guilt, or fear, but instead, with the clarity of love.

That is the pathway to finally releasing that weight.

You don't need to be perfect to feel worthy of love, *especially your own love.* You don't need to have it all figured out.

You don't need to deny anything you've done. You just need to show up for yourself, even when shame tries to tell you that you don't deserve it and should hide yourself away.

All parts of you deserve love, especially the parts that the shame is trying to hide.

So give yourself that love. Don't push your shame away. Hold it. Acknowledge it. Let it be there, thank it for trying to protect you, and then let it move on.

No need to force, control, or fight. It will move. It will dissolve. The more light you shine on it, the more it shrinks naturally.

Love it. It will release.

You Are Not Meant To Carry The Weight Of The World

Have you noticed a tendency to take on more than you can handle?

To think that you have to fix everything, solve everyone's problems, and put the weight of the world on your shoulders as if you alone have to bear that weight. Wow. That's a lot of pressure.

You were *never actually meant to carry the weight of the world.* You really weren't. Nobody expects that of you.

It's okay to put things down, for as long as you need. It's okay to not have to fix everything. It's totally allowed for you to not have a solution and keep being the solution all of the time.

The world doesn't expect you to have all the answers, and you definitely don't need to be doing it all yourself out of some idea that it is required of you in order to feel safe, connected, valued, or loved.

There's always going to be something else or something more to do, but you don't have to be the one to do it all. You're allowed to step back and say, "I need some space", without even giving a reason why.

You are allowed to release some of that pressure. It's okay to lean on others, to ask for help, to admit that you don't have to be in control all the time. You don't need to hold it all together for everyone else.

Trust that it's not all on you. You're allowed to set down the heavy things and give yourself as much time, space, and peace as you need.

You don't have to do it all. You're allowed to take a break, to not have all the answers, to just live in the moment. The weight of the world isn't yours to carry alone. And that's perfectly okay.

It's okay to ask for help. It's okay to share the load. You don't have to do everything by yourself. You're allowed to pass things off to others. To share the load.

When you try to carry everything on your own, you burn out. You exhaust yourself. And that's not the life you deserve.

You deserve balance, peace, and the ability to take care of yourself so that you can offer care to others when it feels right.

So, let go of that unnecessary burden. You don't have to do it all.

It's Okay To Hit The Reset Button

Go for it. Hit reset.

Start again. Start fresh. Whatever happened before, let it go. It is more than okay to reset yourself.

Reset your mind. Reset your body. Reset your decision making. Whatever it means for you to reset, you have every right to let the old just melt away and to start from scratch.

Starting again is not a failure. Not at all. Starting again is just that – starting again. You get to tell the story about whether that is a good or a bad thing. (Hint – you can make it a *good story*). At the end of the day, it really is a good thing to let yourself start fresh.

It's giving yourself a fresh new beginning, and sometimes, you really need that. You need times in your life where you accept that the momentum you had needs to pause for a moment. That the direction you were going needs to change.

That the action and energy you had doesn't need to continue in the same way.

Sometimes, things that used to feel good for us will stop adding value to our lives. When we can be attuned to what feels right and what is creating positive ripple effects in our lives, we can make healthy decisions that bring more value, joy, peace, love, and growth.

You have every right to hit reset on your mind, body, emotions, action, perspective, and life direction.

You can hit reset every 5 minutes if you need to. There is no time too late to reset. There's no time too early to reset. You have the ability to do it at absolutely any time you choose.

Try it right now, if you like. Hit the button, and continue reading...

There's no pressure to continue with something that isn't right anymore. You aren't obliged to keep investing in a direction that isn't true for you anymore.

If you feel off, you can totally go and reset by doing whatever you need to do.

Need to hide from the world? Those bed covers are waiting for you to burrito yourself into. Want to turn off your phone and not talk to anyone for a little while to reset? Do it. Need to take a day off work? Go out in nature? Cry? Whatever you need to do to reset is totally okay, and it's your choice. Every reset will look different.

Hit reset. Hit that button as many times as you need.

You Can Choose Yourself

It's so easy to forget that you can make yourself a priority, isn't it? You make sure everyone else is okay, make sure everyone else is happy, and somewhere along the way, you forget that you're allowed to ask for what you need, too.

You don't always have to be the one who's there for everyone else. You can be there for you, too.

We all want that.

Maybe you've been waiting for someone else to choose you. Maybe you've been choosing everyone else first so that maybe one day they will choose you back.

But it doesn't work that way.

Choosing yourself first is the only way others will truly choose you. It's true, even if it doesn't feel like it right now.

You're allowed to put yourself first without feeling bad about it. You're allowed to take a step back and think, "What do I need right now?" You don't have to apologize for choosing your peace, your energy, your time. It's not selfish. It's necessary.

It's okay if you need space. It's okay to say no when you need to, even if you're worried about letting someone down. You don't have to give and give and give until you're empty. You deserve to be filled up, too.

When you choose yourself, you're not saying you don't care about others. You're reminding yourself that you matter just as much as everyone else. Your needs are just as important as everyone else's, and you don't need to feel guilty for taking care of yourself.

When you choose yourself, people also get permission to choose themselves, too. And that's a beautiful thing. They will start to see that this is actually a healthy way to show up, and that it helps us show up for our relationships with more energy and clearer intention.

You deserve moments where it's all about you. You deserve to take that break and to set that boundary, regardless of whether people like it or not.

You're worthy of all the time, attention, and care. You're worthy of being a priority in your own life.

You don't have to explain yourself. You don't have to justify it. You definitely don't need to earn it.

You are allowed to choose you.

You Are Not
Your Thoughts

Your thoughts don't define you.

Your thoughts happen. Sometimes, they're focused and on purpose, with your intention directing your thoughts. Sometimes, they happen without your effort at all, just background noise or patterns ways they're used to showing up. Sometimes, those thoughts will creep in against what you would really would rather think.

Your mind can be noisy. And even mean, at times. The truth is, sometimes your mind might not be such a nice place to be.

But know that even if your mind is filled with doubt, fear, or negativity about life, or yourself, your thoughts are not YOU. They don't dictate your worth.

And you don't need to be afraid of your thoughts. Even if what happens in your head scares you.

Your thoughts will always come and go, like passing clouds. What matters is what you choose to pay attention to. You get to decide. If you want to pay attention to something other than those thoughts that don't feel nice, you can.

You get to shift your focus. Not to avoid important feelings, but as a way to choose peace. You'll know when it is avoidance or peace.

Ultimately, you are not your thoughts, because you are the one who is observing the thoughts. It takes practice, and overtime, you will get more skilled at it. We all start somewhere, and if this is the start of your journey to reclaiming your power over your thoughts, you're doing great.

You are more than your fears. You are more than your doubts. You are more than the confusion. You are more than any negative thought that crosses your mind. Those thoughts aren't you. They aren't a reflection of who you are.

Those thoughts don't control you. You have the power to acknowledge them, but you don't have to let them define who you are. You don't have to believe every thought.

You are the one who decides what to believe about yourself and about life. How? By seeing the thought, not trying to push it away or get lost in it, but simply observing it without judgment.

You can say, "Hi, thought, I see you. I am not you." It will lose its power. It really will. If you give it no power, it will shrink, so much that it dissolves into nothingness, until a new thought pops up (which it will). Watch those thoughts. Thank them for the messages they're bringing about yourself, your life, and what you need, but know that you don't need to believe every story that comes up in your mind.

They're all just stories.

Make friends with your thoughts. They can help you, bring you amazing insight, solutions, and inspiration. And they can show you where you still have room to grow and heal. Yes, they're not always easy to navigate, but that's okay. Allow them to be as they are, and the hard ones will lose power over you.

Remember who you really are.

You are not your thoughts; you are the spark of consciousness that is able to observe them like passing clouds.

Tap into that power of peace.

Celebrate Your Small Steps

You don't need to wait for the big moments to celebrate yourself. You don't have to accomplish something super grand to give yourself a pat on the back.

Have you been withholding your own support of yourself? Feel like you haven't yet earned it?

It's time to change that, and become your best cheerleader.

It's easy to get caught up in the idea that you need to hit some huge goal to finally feel good about your progress.

But those little steps you take *every day*? They matter. They absolutely matter and are worth celebrating.

Managed to complete one thing off your to-do list? Celebrate it. What about just simply getting out of bed today? Celebrate that, too. Still here, alive and breathing? That's no less deserving of your celebration.

Maybe today wasn't perfect. Maybe you didn't finish everything you wanted to. Maybe you didn't even start it. But you did something. Some small thing – no matter what it was – that counts.

Every little move you make is worth celebrating, because you're showing up. You're making progress. Simply by existing, you are showing up.

It's so easy to forget how far you've come when the finish line feels so far away. But when you take a moment to look at where you started, those small steps start to add up. You're allowed to feel proud of what you've done, no matter how tiny it seems.

You don't need to be constantly achieving big things to be worthy of celebrating. You're worthy right now, just for showing up.

Don't let yourself pass over those moments where you did something – anything – that moves you in the right direction. Even if it's just getting through the day. Even if it's just one small win.

You are taking action, no matter how big or small. No matter what pace that is. I know it feels sometimes you've taken 60 billion steps back. That's okay. Even just noticing that is a cause for celebration.

Every little step you take (especially those that people can't see), the ones that give you more inner peace and support your mental health – they should absolutely be celebrated.

You deserve to be recognized. You are making progress, even if it doesn't feel like it. Those little wins add up. They're all leading you somewhere. And you're allowed to feel good about that.

Don't reserve "feeling good" for only huge moments. Celebrate every tiny little thing. You are allowed to be proud of all things It's *okay* to celebrate small victories.

Right now, those small steps are enough. You're enough. And you deserve your own celebration.

You Are Not Broken

Even if you feel it. Even if you want to give up.

Do you feel like the pieces of you will never get back together? It's understandable to feel that way, but it doesn't mean it is true.

Feel like you're broken beyond repair? It might feel very strong within you that there is no way you could ever be fixed again, but try not to believe that story too strongly right now.

You're full. You are complete. Even in your fragile state. Even in the moments when you feel like you can't take another step. You're still whole.

It's easy to feel like something's wrong with you when things aren't going right.

When everything feels heavy, when you're stuck, when you feel lost. But none of that makes you broken. You're not less than anyone else. You're not behind. You're just in a moment, and that moment will pass. Even if it takes a little while. Maybe it's a long moment.

And maybe there are pieces that have fallen to the ground. Maybe some things did break. But **you** aren't broken. And sometimes things need to fall apart for us to put them back together in a way where they become even more strong and whole.

You're allowed to feel everything you feel – sad, confused, hurt, exhausted. You're allowed to fall apart. That doesn't make you broken. That makes you human. And it makes you someone who is growing, changing, and receptive to all of life – the easy and the hard. The beautiful and the rough.

You're not incomplete. You don't need to fix yourself. You don't need to hide the parts of you that feel broken. People like helping, and they want to help you put things back together.

When you're in that process of putting things back together, remember that you're still not broken. You're just rearranging. Right now, in whatever state you're in, you're enough. You don't have to be perfect. You don't have to have the pieces of your life all perfect, either.

It's okay to be a little messy. It's okay to be fragile. You are not broken. You are whole, just as you are. Even when life isn't perfect, even when things feel tough. You're allowed to take up space.

You're allowed to be where you are; however you are. And none of that changes your worth.

It's Okay To Feel Hurt

It hurts to feel hurt. It's uncomfortable, it's heavy, and it's draining.

And although you might not want to feel it right now, it's okay to feel hurt. You don't need to push it away or pretend you're fine when you're not. It's okay to admit that it hurts. It's okay to just sit with the hurt and not try to do anything with it.

It's okay to feel so hurt you don't know how to go on. It's okay to feel so hurt you're stuck, confused, and unable to see any pathway forward.

How about you just let yourself feel what you feel, and not work it out right now? What about just tending to the hurt softly, gently, with kindness?

You don't have to have all the answers right now. You don't have to understand why it hurts or figure out how to fix it. It's okay to just let it hurt. Let it be there. You don't have to justify it or explain it to anyone. They might try to force an explanation from you, or even try to take away your hurt in ways that don't help. It's also true that some people may even try to hurt you more.

But that doesn't mean that you need to let anyone make you feel worse, or make you feel that your hurt isn't valid. Including yourself. You feel what you feel and it's not bad that you feel things that aren't always sunshiny and light.

You're not wrong, bad, weak, or silly for feeling hurt. You're not undeserving of being heard, cared for, and supported in your hurt. If others' can't offer that, it's not about you. You are deserving of being held in your hurt, even if you're the only one who can hold you right now.

You don't have to be over it. You don't need to rush through it. If it hurts, you're allowed to feel that. It's okay to not have it all figured out. It's okay to not be okay. You don't have to change how you feel to make anyone else comfortable, while you push down what is true for you.

Let it be true. It doesn't mean the hurt will consume you, or always be there. It doesn't mean that you won't ever get over it. You're allowed to admit that it hurts right now, and know that eventually it will move and change and not hurt as much later on. Try not to be afraid of the hurt. Let it exist.

You don't need to fall into the pit of hurt and bring more hurt onto yourself with stories that feel damaging, but you also don't need to push it all to the side in denial.

It's okay to just be in this moment. You're allowed to feel everything you're feeling, as messy and raw as it may be. You don't have to move past it yet. You're allowed to be here.

You don't need to bounce back or get over it. It's okay to hurt. It's okay to just exist in it. Sometimes, hurt just happens. And it's okay to feel it.

It's okay to take up space with your hurt. You don't have to hide it. You don't have to shrink yourself because you're hurting. You are allowed to be in this. You are allowed to feel everything you're feeling.

None of that takes away from who you are. You're still you. You're still whole. Even in your hurt.

You Don't Have To Be Ashamed Of Your Darkness

Your darkness isn't weakness. It's not bad. It's not wrong. And you don't need to hide it.

Your darkness isn't something to be ashamed of.

You are lovable, even with your darkness. You are wanted. You are worthy. Your darkness doesn't make you less valuable. It doesn't make you less deserving of being treated with kindness and care.

You don't need to lock down the dark parts of you and throw the key away.

You don't need to be scared that the darkness will take over (even though it feels like that sometimes). It's okay if you feel overwhelmed by the darker parts of you, and it's okay that they might feel threatening and intimidating.

You are safe to have darkness.

You are safe to share your darkness. You aren't the only one who battles in the dark. You aren't alone in struggling with the darker parts of you. It's something that connects us all, even when it feels totally and utterly lonely.

It doesn't mean that there is no light within you, either. There is still light. Even when it is so dark that all you can see is nothingness. The light is still there, and will be lit again. The darkness won't consume you if you let go of the shame.

Actually, it releases some of the tension and heaviness of the darkness, when you accept it.

Right now, breathe some softness to your darkness. I know you want to shut it down. I know you don't want it to pull you down anymore. I know it's been hard, and continues to be hard to manage.

You're okay. As you are, in this darkness. Your darkness is accepted. It is worthy of being validated. You don't need to slip into it, and let it rule you. You can see it with kind eyes. You can observe it with curiosity, even if it still hurts, notice how you can look at your darkness. Notice how you can learn from it.

And notice then, that you aren't the darkness; you are the one who is observing the darkness.

And maybe, just maybe, things seem a little less dark when you notice that.

Let Go Of Who You Thought You Were

You don't need to hold onto that version of yourself anymore.

It's okay to let it go.

It's okay to let it fall away. Some people might want to try to latch onto it, because it makes them feel better for you to stay that way. Maybe it makes them feel a certain way about themselves if you stayed the same. But you don't owe that to them.

Staying attached to an old version of you that really doesn't feel like who you are anymore is not benefiting anyone.

You are worth letting it go.

You don't have to keep being that person you thought you were meant to be. You're allowed to change. You're allowed to grow. And you're allowed to let go of who you thought you were, regardless of anyone else's feelings and thoughts about it.

You don't need to stay stuck in the past version of you. That version is only a memory. When you realize that you are not that person anymore, the only thing left to do is to let go of the *idea that the past you is the real you now.*

You're already a different version of you, actually. All that is left is to say goodbye to that memory.

You deserve to grow and let go.

Whatever stories you held about who you thought you were and you who thought you should be; **they are only stories.** You can rewrite them. Right now. And at any moment, you can keep rewriting. Again and again, rewrite who you are.

You get to choose who you are and how you show up. People may cling to the old version of you, and keep you in their minds as that. That's okay. Let them. You know who you are. That's enough.

It's okay if you feel different. It's okay if you're not who you thought you'd be. You don't need to live up to who you imagined you would become. You're allowed to be someone new.

You're allowed to change your mind, change your values and beliefs, your direction, and change your whole life if you need to. You don't have to be that person you once thought you had to be. You get to choose who you are right now.

Let go. You don't have to hold on to any old version of yourself.

You get to move forward, free from who you thought you were.

It's Okay to
Ask For Space

You have every right to ask for space. That is your birthright.

Whether it is space from communicating with someone, space from a responsibility you've been holding for a while, physical space for yourself to rest, or space from a difficult situation.

You don't have to keep pushing yourself to be there for everyone all the time. You don't have to be "on" all of the time. You don't have to always give and give. You don't have to always show up.

If you need space, you're allowed to take it. Without any explanation.

You're allowed to step back, even if it feels uncomfortable or even a little selfish.

You don't have to justify it or apologize for it. You don't owe anyone your energy all the time. Your peace is important.

Sometimes, you need to create that space for yourself, despite how others feel about it. Asking for space is respecting others in the process, even if they can't see that.

There will be moments, too, where the space you need won't be asked for, but taken. Where there is no one to ask, and only you to give it to yourself.

Sometimes, you will ask for space and someone will not have the capacity and understanding to see how much it is needed, and they won't want to agree. And even when that happens, you are 100% allowed to take the space, anyway. No agreement needed on their part. That's your right.

You're allowed to feel like you've given everything you can and you just need a break.

That's okay. It doesn't mean you're not there for others or that you're failing in some way. It means you're taking care of yourself, and that's the only way you can actually go back out there and show up how you want to show up.

Don't feel bad for needing a little distance. It's okay to say, "I need a moment."

You don't have to be available for everything. You don't have to be available for everyone. And you certainly don't have to be available when you're not ready.

Firstly, be available for yourself. You deserve to ask for space.

You Are Allowed To Be A Mess

It's okay to be all over the place. It's okay to feel confused and overwhelmed. It's okay to feel not yourself; not balanced, not peaceful, and not clear. Even more than that, it's okay if you feel like a total mess.

Be a mess.

Seriously. Let yourself be messy. It doesn't make you any less worthy. It doesn't make you any less valuable. It doesn't make you wrong or unlikable.

It's okay if things aren't perfect, if your mind feels cluttered, if everything around you feels like it's falling apart, or if you feel like you're falling apart. You don't need to apologize for feeling like a mess. You don't need to hide it. You're allowed to have no idea which way is up or down.

You're allowed to be messy, and you are allowed to be accepted for that.

You absolutely deserve to be accepted when you're messy.

You don't need to keep pretending that you are all clean and perfect. That you are shiny and put together, when you feel anything but that.

You can stop pretending that you're feeling something that you aren't. You don't need to play a character of cleanliness when it's not true for you right now.

You don't have to have it all figured out. You don't need to keep pretending everything is fine when it's not.

You don't need to put on a brave face when you're struggling. If you're a mess right now, that's more than okay. You're still worthy of love and care. You're still enough.

It's normal to think you have to have everything together to be acceptable, to be loved, or to be seen as strong. But you don't. You don't need to have everything perfectly arranged or perfectly planned or perfectly presented. Be confused, unsure, tired, or overwhelmed.

Fwhatever you feel.

You don't need to clean all the mess up before you're allowed to take a break. You don't need to have all the answers, or the perfect solutions for you to accept yourself.

You're allowed to feel lost, to feel frustrated, and to feel like you're just trying to get through the day. You're allowed to feel all of that and still give yourself love.

You don't have to be perfect to deserve peace. You don't need to be succeeding in your life to be worthy of rest. You don't need to keep it together just because society tells you to. You are allowed to just *be*—messy, raw, real—and still be whole.

Your mess doesn't take away from who you are. In fact, it's part of what makes you real, and that's beautiful.

You Are Not Alone In Your Struggles

It can feel so isolating when you're in the thick of it, when everything feels like it's falling apart and it seems like no one else could possibly understand what you're going through.

Even when you feel like you're stuck in your head, as if the world is moving on around you while you're standing still stuck in your struggles, you are not alone.

There are people who've been where you are. There are people who get it, even if you can't see them right now. You don't have to carry it by yourself. You don't have to face it all alone. You get to ask for support. You deserve to receive support.

You can share your struggles with others, and let yourself be heard. You are not a burden to someone because you share your difficulties.

You are not alone. When you let others in, you'll see just how much support is out there waiting for you.

There's strength in knowing that even when you feel like you're drowning in your struggles, there are others who understand. You might not know them yet, but they're out there, walking through their own storms just like you.

Maybe there are people in your life who you can think of right now that would be able to relate to your struggles. You might be surprised at the people you thought were "put together" and never had any issues of their own who can actually relate to you.

You're not alone in how you feel.

You're not the only one battling your inner demons, your fears, or your pain. There is comfort in knowing others share this journey. You can embrace this comfort now, and let it warm you. Because you aren't alone.

Others might also be able to share some comforting words, or even just silent company in being with you, to show you how not alone you really are. But even if there isn't anyone for you right now, you can rest in the knowledge that you truly aren't alone in your struggles, and what you're feeling is not wrong or bad.

It doesn't make you weak to feel these hard moments. You are human, and these hard moments are inevitable.

You're allowed to reach out and to share what's on your heart. You're allowed to ask for help when you're feeling like you can't do it all. You don't have to keep everything bottled up. You don't have to pretend you're okay when you're not.

It's okay to lean on others. You do not have to struggle in silence. There's no shame in needing support. There's no weakness in asking for someone to be there for you.

People want to be there for you, even strangers.

You are not alone in your struggles. You have never been.

You Don't Have To Please Everyone

Hey. Guess what? You can stop trying to make everyone else happy at your expense.

You don't owe anyone your time, your energy, your peace, or your comfort just to make them feel good. You do not need to twist yourself into knots to fit into their version of who you *should be.*

You are allowed to love the feeling of making people feel happy. It feels beautiful to know we can have that effect on people. But to compromise yourself to please someone else – that never ends well. It never creates the peace we think it will.

Recall some moments where you put your all into pleasing others, at the expense of your peace... Did it actually make you feel good?

Nope. It doesn't bring goodness.

You are not here to serve everyone else. And if you are chasing the feeling of value you get from pleasing someone, know that you are valuable as a human without pleasing everyone. Let go of the fear of being ridiculed for speaking your truth and needs.

Sure, you won't be able to make everyone happy all of the time, but that's theirs to navigate, not yours. You aren't responsible for their feelings.

Speaking your truth and needs is a gift you give to yourself, and people will either accept, or they won't. That's the simple truth that you can't control.

You are not here to be whatever they need you to be, at the expense of your own authenticity and happiness. You don't need to be constantly "on," constantly saying yes, constantly putting on a character to try to "keep the peace." You are not their puppet. You are not existing to be convenient for others.

It's understandable that you feel that you might lose love, connection, belonging, and peace, if you stop trying to make everyone happy. After all, this belief came from somewhere. But you get to rewrite this story now. You get to decide whether you keep living this way.

You know what people respect? Boundaries. They truly do respect seeing another person be clear in their yes and no. When people see you valuing yourself, they see you as a higher value. It's true. And it is not by self-sacrificing that you reach that feeling of respect from others.

It's exhausting. Running around trying to meet everyone's needs, trying to make them happy, and losing yourself in the process. But remember this; You don't have to be the one who keeps things together for them.

You don't have to mold yourself into whatever they want you to be.

You're allowed to stop caring so much about who likes you. You can stop stressing over who accepts you.

You don't have to be liked by everyone. You don't have to be accepted by everyone. Someone doesn't gel with you? That's *perfectly fine*. Because you don't like every single person anyway, right? You don't fully gel with all people either. And that's okay.

If someone gets upset, so be it. That's not your problem. If someone doesn't understand why you're choosing to put yourself first, that's their issue to work through, not yours. You don't need to apologize for needing space. You don't need to justify your boundaries. You're allowed to choose *you* without feeling guilty,

Your purpose is not to please everyone. You are not here to be their everything. You are here to be *you*, unapologetically.

You can stop shrinking yourself. Stop apologizing for existing as you are. You don't have to please anyone. Let them please themselves. Give them that job. Pass it back to them. It was always their responsibility, anyway. Just as your happiness is your responsibility.

You only have to be true to yourself. And the beauty of that is, there will be so many people who adore you as you are, without you needing to put effort into people pleasing your way into their good graces. They will simply value you exactly as you are.

It starts with you valuing and respecting yourself.

Slowing Down
Is Okay

It really is 100% okay to slow down.

Let that pace settle into a slower rhythm, one where you're no longer driven by erratic energy, hustle, and haste. However slow that rhythm is, it's perfect.

No one says you have to be moving at a million miles per hour all the time. (Except maybe that voice in your head). But guess what?

You can quiet that voice down, and decide to do something differently. You really do have the power to make a different decision about the pace you are taking your life.

You can take your foot off the gas and still be moving forward. You can accomplish your goals at a slower pace. You really can.

The world might push you to keep going, to never stop, to always hustle—but that doesn't have to be your rule. You're allowed to slow down and breathe.

You're allowed to slow down so much that you stop for a bit.

The constant rush, the pressure to keep up, it's exhausting. And it's easy to feel guilty for wanting to pause and rest. It's easy to feel like you haven't yet earned the rest. But the truth is, taking your time is a strength, not a weakness.

You don't lose anything by stepping back. In fact, you gain perspective. You rejuvenate. You give yourself greater clarity through this small act of self-care.

A lot of the time, you're even more intentional, productive, and successful in what you do when you slow down, too. It's ironic but sometimes you get to your goal faster when you go slower.

If you're feeling worn out, it's not a sign of failure. It's a sign that you're human. You're not built to run on empty. Letting yourself slow down means you're giving yourself the space to refuel.

You can move at your own pace and still get where you need to be.

You're not falling behind just because you're taking a moment to rest. The world's idea of productivity isn't your standard. There's no prize for running yourself into the ground. Slowing down isn't even about doing less, it's about doing what you need.

It's about tuning in and deciding to give yourself a break and take it down a notch.

Taking a step back is not just okay, it's necessary. Pause and just *be* without the guilt. You're allowed to exist at your pace, however slow it is.

Don't buy into the pressure to keep moving when you need to rest. You'll get there. But first, take a moment. Slow down.

And give yourself permission to simply live at whatever pace feels right.

You Don't Have To Apologize For Being Happy

Do you feel like you need to downplay your happiness? Like you have to shrink yourself when things are going well?

Maybe you're afraid it will make others feel worse to see you happy if they are not feeling great right now. Maybe you have hurt others in the past and made mistakes, and don't feel worthy of true happiness until you are sufficiently punished.

But the truth is you don't have to feel guilty for being happy, for having moments that are light and for enjoying the things in life. You deserve to feel that way, no matter what you have done in the past.

No matter what you did, said, and who you were in the past... You still deserve happiness, and you never have to apologize for it.

It's okay to be happy, even when the world around you isn't perfect. You're allowed to enjoy your life, even when there is pain and suffering. It's okay to feel good, to smile, and to laugh. You don't need to dim your light or make yourself smaller just because someone else is struggling or because things aren't perfect.

Your happiness doesn't take away from anyone else's.

It's the opposite, actually. Your happiness can be a gift for others. It can lighten their own darkness.

You don't need to apologize for feeling joy, especially if it's a small thing. If it's something that feels "insignificant," it doesn't make it any less important for you. It is worth being happy about anything that really does give you joy. All of it matters.

It's okay to be excited about what you love, to celebrate the things that make you feel good, and to share that with people in your life. You don't have to hide it. And you definitely don't have to apologize for it.

Take up space with your joy.

Joy is welcome. And you'll see how people want to be in that space with you – you'll feel how people are magnetized to it. You'll start to see that your happiness is a superpower.

It's yours. Own it.

You're Not Weak

Just because you're struggling doesn't mean something is wrong with you.

You're allowed to be tired. You're allowed to not have it all figured out. You're allowed to feel like you're not okay. Feeling weak right now doesn't make you any less than anyone else.

You don't need to have it together all the time to be strong. You're allowed to have moments when you're not at your best. That's not weakness. That's life.

Struggling doesn't mean you're weak.

Not being able to show up perfectly isn't weak.

If you can't match your standards from yesterday, you're still not weak.

And the truth is, feeling weak doesn't mean that you are weak.

You don't have to keep pushing yourself until you break. It's okay to admit that things are tough, to share that you're struggling, and to acknowledge that you need a minute. You're human.

You might think everyone else looks so strong, so why can't you be like that? The ones who act like they're fine all the time? They're the ones who are avoiding the truth that they, too, struggle sometimes.

You're not weak for being real. In fact, it's the complete opposite. The strength is in *owning* where you are and being okay with it. It takes courage to be honest about where you're at.

The greatest irony is that there is only strength when you say "I feel weak right now." That is a bold move.

When you feel overwhelmed, when you feel like you can't go on, when you feel defeated – remember, it doesn't make you weak. It means you're feeling what you're feeling. Full stop. You don't need to hide that or suppress it to prove anything to anyone (including yourself).

You're allowed to not have everything figured out. You're allowed to feel lost and fragile. You're allowed to ask for help. You're allowed to rest. These aren't signs of weakness.

You're here, feeling your feelings, doing the work. That's power.

You're not weak. You're real.

Others' Emotions Are Not Your Responsibility

Their feelings are not yours to fix. If they are upset, angry, sad, or hurt, that's on them, *not you.*

You don't need to apologize for how they feel. You don't need to adjust yourself, change your actions, or swallow your truth just to make them more comfortable. You can admit your role in the situation, if you truly did have a role in it, but you are not responsible for the feelings that they are having about what has happened.

It's not your job to manage their emotions. You are allowed to live your life without taking on their baggage. If they're in a bad mood, you don't need to absorb it. If they're angry, that's not your fault.

You're not the keeper of their happiness. You don't have to tiptoe around their feelings to avoid conflict. You don't have to make yourself smaller just to make someone feel better. You don't need to show how guilty you are. That's not going to solve anyway.

You don't need to fix them, and you don't need to feel responsible for their reactions. If they're upset, let them be upset. That's theirs, not yours. You're allowed to live your life, set your boundaries, and protect your peace.

Stay accountable for your actions, have empathy for their experience, and let go of the rest. You're allowed to exist without worrying about how other people feel or how their emotions are affecting you.

Stop internalizing other people's moods. You don't need to carry their emotional weight. You don't need to make things better for them. You can want that, sure. You want others to be happy, of course. But it's not yours to manage.

Their feelings are theirs. You are not responsible for them. And that's more than okay.

It's important to take care of yourself first. You're allowed to be true to yourself, even if it makes someone else uncomfortable. You don't need to apologize for your feelings, your boundaries, or the way you show up in the world. If someone else feels upset and tries to make you the reason why they're upset, you have the choice to believe that story or not.

You're able to take responsibility for your actions, whilst not absorbing their energy. You can be sorry for any hurt caused by your actions, without taking on their emotions.

You're not responsible for how other people react to you. You can't control that. What you can control is how you respond and how you choose to act.

You don't need to bear their load in order to show up differently. You don't need to carry their feelings on your shoulders to become a "better person" next time.

It's okay to walk away from situations that make you feel drained. It's okay to let people feel what they feel without making it yours. You don't need to make it better for them. You don't need to change to suit their emotional needs.

You are responsible for your own peace. For your own well-being. Let them learn to be responsible for theirs.

It's Okay If You Want To Give Up

You don't have to keep fighting. You don't have to keep pushing yourself when it's too much. It's okay to be tired. It's okay to feel like you've hit your limit and can't keep going.

You don't have to pretend to be strong all the time. You don't have to force yourself to keep going just because others expect you to.

I know it seems like you aren't allowed to give up, but you are. It doesn't have to be a negative thing.

You're allowed to be done. You're allowed to say, "I can't do this anymore." It's not weak. It's not a failure. It's just *real*. You're human. And humans get tired. They reach their breaking points. That's okay. Let yourself reach that point, if that's where you are.

Why not change the definition of "giving up" to simply "letting go"?

You don't need to keep going if it's draining you.

You don't have to push through every single thing, especially when you've given it your all. It's okay to let go when something no longer serves you when it's taking more from you than you can give.

It's also okay to give up even when part of you still wants to keep going. Maybe you invested a lot of time, energy, attention, money, love, hope... And to give up now would feel like it has all been wasted. That's understandable.

But it hasn't been a waste. All of your experiences have added to your life – whether positive or negative. You have learned, grown, and little-by-little, kept moving forward.

It's really okay to throw the towel in. Even if others have some judgments about that. Let them. You don't have to take on their judgments. You don't owe anyone an explanation for why you're giving up. You don't need to justify your feelings. If you want to give up, that's your right. Let yourself.

Give up right now if you want to. Go for it. I'm not judging. And you don't have to judge yourself. You're not broken. You're not weak.

You're just being real with yourself in what you need, what you want, and what your limits are. Give up, start again, let yourself find your own way. It's all okay.

You Can Walk
Away

Right now, you can walk away.

No explanation. No reason. No convincing anyone why it's what you need and want.

You don't need to have any reason to walk away

If you know that it would feel best to walk away, then do it. Walk away. You don't owe anyone a justification. You can stay 100% silent about it if you choose to. You can share the reasons why, if you want to.

Whatever it is that you are walking away from, you are allowed that. You don't have to stay because you owe something to someone or to a situation.

If it means to continue to compromise yourself and your peace and health, there is nothing more important than claiming this peace back by walking away.

You don't owe anyone your time, your energy, or your peace if it's costing you too much. If something isn't serving you, you are allowed to walk away. If it's draining you and if it's not right for you anymore, it's okay to walk away. If it simply just doesn't feel right anymore, you are absolutely allowed to walk away.

You don't have to stay in situations that make you uncomfortable, unhappy, or unappreciated. You don't need to suffer in a situation that feels empty or unfulfilling (even if you don't know why).

You're allowed to leave, even if it feels hard. You certainly don't have to feel guilty for taking care of yourself.

You don't have to stay where you're not wanted. You don't have to stay where you're not valued. You're allowed to walk away, even if you feel fear or hesitation (that's totally normal).

Is your loyalty keeping you there? If loyalty is keeping you somewhere that is making you feel distressed or depleted, then what are you really loyal to? The distress?

Be loyal to your needs. Be loyal to self-respect. There are going to be moments where that means walking away is the best thing you can do.

It's okay to walk away from relationships, jobs, situations, or places that don't align with your values and who you are anymore. You're allowed to move on, to choose a different path, and to step away from anything you decide to. It's your life, and you get to design it your way.

Free yourself of the obligation and guilt. You can walk away peacefully. It doesn't have to be a big dramatic action. It can be a silent stepping away, if that is what you wish.

Know that It's okay to close that door and walk toward something that feels better, even if that means walking alone for a while. You also don't need to have the next step figured out yet.

Walking away isn't a sign of weakness. It's a sign of strength.

Choosing yourself is always the right choice. So, if that means you need to walk away, let yourself.

You'll Outgrow Old Versions Of Yourself

It's inevitable.

You are always outgrowing the old you – every single day.

Outgrowing old versions of yourself is already happening, it's just that sometimes we don't like to admit it. We think we should stay the same, and letting go of the old you isn't always a pleasant experience, so sometimes we really try to stay the same because it feels more comfortable.

But the truth is, you're not meant to stay the same. You're not meant to be stuck in who you were yesterday, last year, or five years ago. And it isn't actually more comfortable to stay frozen in time.

You outgrew your 5-year-old self, right? So, why wouldn't you also outgrow who you were last year? Or last week? Or yesterday?

You are always evolving. You're always growing, little-by-little, every moment of every day (even if it feels like you are taking five steps back). The person you used to be isn't the person you are now, and it won't be the person who you show up as tomorrow.

Outgrowing old versions of yourself is beautiful. It shows that you're not stuck. You're not locked into a stagnant state of being. Accepting that you will outgrow who you thought you were is a step towards greater peace and balance in your life.

Maybe it'll be sad, sometimes. Maybe you want to hold onto the old you. It's normal to feel that way, but know that the new you is a little wiser, with more life experience, more hindsight, and perhaps more empathy and patience. Even more capacity for love.

You can try to hold onto old habits, old beliefs, and old versions of yourself. But ultimately, it's a losing battle because you're meant to grow. You're meant to shed the skin of who you once were and step into something new, even if it's uncomfortable.

It's supposed to feel like you're leaving parts of yourself behind. Because you are. It'll feel strange and maybe sad. Let yourself feel that, and know that you can keep moving forward into the new versions of who you are and will be.

You don't have to stay who you were just because it's familiar. You don't owe the past you anything. You don't have to keep holding onto things that held you back just because you've been carrying them for so long. And you don't need to prove to anyone else that you're "still the same person." Because – newsflash – you're not.

Anyone who requires you to stay in an old version of you for them to be happy is not meant to stay in your life. Sadly, there will be relationships that may not be able to continue on in this new path you are taking in life.

You may have to let go of more than just your old self. You may also have to let go of things that this version of yourself wanted. What they believed. Who they spent time with. Who their friends were... And that's hard.

But if they truly don't fit anymore, *let them go.*

It's not weak to change. It's not wrong to outgrow who you used to be. In fact, it's the whole point. You are not meant to stay in the same place, repeating the same cycles. You are meant to shift, to grow, to become more of who you really are by rediscovering yourself the more you shed the old layers.

And when this new version of you looks and feels different, that's something to celebrate.

You don't need to keep holding yourself back by latching onto the image of who you used to be. Because who you used to be doesn't exist anymore. It's time to embrace the change. Embrace the new you.

You are exactly where you need to be, and tomorrow, you'll be even further along.

You Are Not
A Failure
For Changing
Directions

Do you think that once you've committed to something, that's it? That you're stuck? That if you turn around or make a new choice, it means you didn't try hard enough?

Or it means that you're a failure?

Do you believe that if you really did change direction now, it would prove a negative story you have about yourself?

It's understandable to feel that way, but it's not true.

Changing your mind doesn't make you a failure – it makes you someone who knows when something isn't working and takes action. And that's strength. That's wisdom.

You're allowed to change your mind. Knowing that something is not working and that a shift is needed is not failure.

That's honesty. You're giving yourself the chance to do better, to choose a path that actually aligns with who you are now. And to try something else that may or may not work out.

That is a wise power to be proud of.

You don't need to keep forcing yourself down a road that doesn't feel right. If you've gotten caught up in the sunk-cost fallacy – believing you've invested too much time, energy, or resources to turn back, know that no investment is lost.

It's okay if you've spent a lot to get to where you are, and changing direction now doesn't make any of that a waste. You're now just on the next step of your journey.

You learned what works and what doesn't. You received more data on what you want and need. And maybe it was a great investment at the time, but now it is simply not for you anymore.

It's okay if it's hard. By changing directions, you have to admit some things that pride doesn't want us to admit. It wants us to stay rooted and loyal to *the plan*. But think about it: the most successful plans are those that are agile.

The ones that can adapt and shift as needed. Just like the strongest tree is the one that can bend with the wind.

You're allowed to let go of what isn't working, even if it feels hard. Even if it feels like you're giving up. You're not giving up. You're making room for something better.

You can stop holding on out of pride or guilt, now. You don't need to keep pushing forward just because you said you would. You're allowed to make a U-turn. As many times as you need. You're allowed to choose yourself over the path you thought you had to take.

There's no shame in reevaluating, in reassessing, and in choosing to move in a different direction. That's not failure. That's what growth looks like.

Be proud of being strong enough to change directions, especially in the face of people who will tell you to stay on the same path.

When you feel like you've made a wrong turn or wasted time, or that you've gone too far to change directions now, remember this: you're not failing. You're evolving. You're doing exactly what you're supposed to do.

You're choosing what's best for you, and that is something you can celebrate.

Well done. **You're doing amazing.**

You Don't Have To Keep Hustling

There's this idea that success is all about hustle and non-stop work.

Do you feel it?

That you need to do more, be more, achieve more, go faster, and keep up with everyone else so that you can finally be happy?

What if success wasn't about being busy all the time? What if success wasn't the gift at the end of the hustle spiral? What if it were about being intentional with your time, aligning your actions with your values, and prioritizing what truly matters to you?

You can be successful without sacrificing your health, your happiness, or your peace. Hustling doesn't have to be the answer. You can achieve great things without running yourself into the ground.

You can reach your goals slowly. It's not the pace that matters, it's the presence you bring to it. And most of the time, hustling skips past important steps and has you unable to even enjoy the steps you're taking.

You can stop running now. Give yourself the permission to step away from the endless grind. You don't need to be in constant motion, always chasing something, always doing more, and proving to the world that you aren't lazy.

The hustle culture wants you to believe that if you're not constantly moving, you're falling behind. But guess what? That's a lie. You don't have to keep hustling to prove you're worthy, to prove you're successful, or to prove you matter. You have nothing to prove to yourself.

You don't need to keep pushing just because everyone else is. There's no badge of honor in exhaustion. No trophy for never stopping.

And your success isn't dependent on how much hustle it took to get you there, as if more hustle equaled more success.

You're not here to exhaust yourself for the sake of productivity. You're here to live. To breathe. To enjoy every moment that exists, not just those short moments of rest when you reach a goal before you hustle to the next.

Hustling harder is not how you win. It's how you burn out. You're allowed to stop. You're allowed to rest.

You don't need to apologize for taking a break and changing pace. You are not defined by how many hours you work or how much you do.

You are more than your productivity.

If you're tired, take a nap. If you're burnt out, stop. If you're overwhelmed, let yourself do absolutely nothing. You don't have to keep pushing yourself until you break. You don't need to run yourself ragged to feel worthy of success. You're allowed to rest.

You're allowed to slow down. Not because you've earned it, but because you deserve it right now.

Your value isn't in how much you do or what you achieve. Your value is in *you*, just as you are.

Stop chasing. Start living. You don't have to keep hustling. You'll get to where you're going, no matter what pace you decide to take.

Let Yourself
Fail

Radical idea: Why don't you just let yourself fail? Seriously.
Give up, and give up so hard that it is a total failure.

Sounds scary, right?

It's the one thing we've all been conditioned to avoid. Fail,
and you're done. Fail, and you're not good enough. Fail, and
it's over.

We're told to keep going, push through, don't accept failure.
But what if you did accept that things didn't work out the
way you planned? Would the sky fall?

Failure is learning. And it will happen. You're allowed to fail.
You're allowed to lose, to look stupid, and not to get it right.

Failure is not the enemy. It's the teacher.

You won't learn how to rise if you never let yourself fall.
You won't get stronger if you're too afraid to fail. You won't
realize what you want, what you need, and what doesn't

work if you don't let yourself fail – or at least even consider the possibility of failing.

You gain a lot through failure, actually. You gain humility, empathy, wisdom, important data to help you move forward... And so much more.

Here's a secret – success isn't always the best teacher. It's a beautiful feeling to succeed, but it's not where resilience is built.

Failing doesn't make you less. It doesn't make you unworthy. It makes you human and it gives you an amazing opportunity to expand. It makes you someone who's brave enough to try, someone who's bold enough to risk it all and still keep moving forward.

That is something to be proud of.

You're not meant to be perfect. You're meant to be messy, real, and willing to stumble. It's in the falling where the magic happens. It's in the failure where the growth happens. Let yourself fail and watch how much stronger you get.

Fail dramatically, and maybe even see if you can enjoy it.

You don't need to pretend that you're flawless. Let go of the fear. Let go of the shame. Failure can be your friend.

If and when you fail – *and you will fail* – be proud of it. Be proud of yourself for trying. Because, the only real failure is not trying at all.

The irony is that by embracing failure, you're already on the path to greater success.

You Deserve To Feel Cherished

Not just loved in the easy ways.

Not just loved when it's convenient for others.

Not just loved for your positive attributes.

You deserve to be adored. You deserve to be the one some-one is grateful and excited to make space for, to take care of, to show up for in every way that counts. You deserve that not because you've done hard work to earn it.

You deserve it because you are worth being cherished. For you being you. As you are.

You don't have to earn affection. You deserve affection right now, as you are. You don't have to prove you're worth the effort. You are. Period.

You should never need to convince anyone of your value. Anyone who needs to be convinced should be immediately removed from your life. They're not able to see themselves with value, so it will make it very difficult to see you in the value you hold. That's okay. Sad. But it's okay that they leave your life, because you deserve more.

You deserve to be valued just for being you. You deserve to have your presence celebrated. You're not here to be someone else's afterthought.

You're not here to be put on the back burner. And you certainly should never accept being treated without respect and care. If you are receiving that treatment, it's time to do all you can to let go of these people and walk away from these situations.

You should never have to endure disrespect and being treated without care by others – even if you understand that they are acting this way because they are wounded. No wounding entitles anyone to mistreat you. And you would be mistreating yourself if you allowed it.

No one has a right to treat you without dignity. You deserve to be prioritized, to be held in high regard, to be seen as something rare and precious.

You are worthy of love, kindness, and attention that makes you feel alive. You deserve to be treated with the same respect, care, and tenderness that you give to others.

You deserve to feel cherished. You deserve to be adored, deeply and unapologetically. And if you're not feeling that now, don't settle. Hold out for the kind of love that makes you feel *worthy*.

Because you are. And you always have been.

Give Your
Inner Critic
Love

You know that voice in your head, the one that tells you you're not good enough, that you're not doing enough, that you'll never be enough?

That voice is loud. It's harsh. It's relentless.

But here's the thing: you don't have to fight it. You don't have to silence it or shove it away.

Give it love instead.

It sounds counter-intuitive – to give a mean voice love. To speak with this voice with tenderness, especially when it is treating you with harshness.

But that voice doesn't exist to destroy you – it exists because it wants you to grow and it doesn't know how else to change your behavior and help you expand. That voice was born many, many years ago. It learned that it needed to criticize you in order for you to adjust your behavior.

In moments you didn't fully show up in line with your values, or when you knew you would have done something differently, or when you didn't quite succeed as you thought you could, that voice tried to fix it. And maybe that voice comes in moments that feel completely unwelcome, to simply compare you with others, tell nasty stories about yourself, and make you feel not good enough.

That voice is misguided, but it doesn't have malicious intentions. Not really. Deep down, it is only saying what it learned to say. It is only repeating a script it heard a long time ago, probably from the people around it that were saying similar things to you, or someone else, or even themselves.

That voice has learned patterns that aren't actually helpful or effective, and it needs time to unlearn them. Be patient with yourself.

Pushing it away and making that voice wrong is not going to help the voice unlearn. It will shut the voice down for some time, but it will come back again. Louder, usually. With more force, and sometimes more hardness, giving you more pain.

So, don't shut the voice down. Don't try to ignore it. Acknowledge it. Look at it and say, "I hear you. I know you're trying to protect me, but I am safe without listening to you." Tell it that you know that what it is saying is coming from a place of deep, deep desire to grow, expand, or even simply feel belonging and connection. Give it love.

It's trying hard. It's not doing so well, but it is trying. Love it for what it is, a part of you that's trying to keep you safe, even if it's doing a terrible job at it.

The key is not to fight your inner critic, but to show it compassion. Show yourself compassion. Remind yourself that you don't have to be perfect, and you don't have to meet impossible standards.

Remind yourself that even if you have a mean inner critic, you aren't mean. Even if you aren't always supportive to yourself, it doesn't mean you don't have the capacity to be supportive.

You're allowed to be human, to make mistakes, and to fail. You're allowed to not always be perfect, and that includes how perfect you are at giving your inner critic love.

It's an unlearning and relearning process. It will take time. You're not worthless. You're not failing. You're not wrong. You're not bad. You're doing the damn best you can. And some days, the best you can is just making it through the day.

Next time your inner critic starts speaking, don't dismiss it. Don't hate it. Don't buy into the stories it's telling you, either. Just see it. Love it. Acknowledge it, sit with it, and then let it move into the background. Remind it that you're fine, that you're enough, just as you are and that you don't need it to try to change you.

You don't need to be perfect to be worthy. Love that voice, because it is just a wounded part that needs to be guided into healing.

And every part of you deserves love.

You Deserve
Time For
Yourself

No guilt. No apologies. No earning it by accomplishing something else first. You deserve the space to just *be*, right now.

You deserve all the time to yourself that you want and need. All of it.

You are allowed to ask for it. You are allowed to tell people that you need to take it. And you don't have to justify why. No explanations are needed. Not proving to anyone why you deserve it.

You don't owe anyone your energy, your time, your focus, or your care 24/7. You're allowed to take a step back and breathe without feeling like you're falling short or letting someone down.

People will understand that you need time for you. And even if people don't understand, that doesn't take away the value and importance for owning your right to claim your space. That is your birthright. No matter what anyone thinks or says.

It's easy to feel like you have to be everything to everyone all the time. It's so easy to get caught in the trap of giving everyone your time and energy. Caring for others feels good. Interacting with people you love feels good. But that doesn't mean that you shouldn't need to step away sometimes.

Everyone needs their space, whatever that looks like. You need that space, and you are the only one who can claim that.

Waiting for someone else to give you that isn't going to help. Sure, they might try to help you see that rest is needed, but it's not up to them to grant you that. It's up to you.

Do you feel sometimes that if you take a moment for yourself, you're being selfish? It's absolutely not. But even if you define it as selfish, you know what? Be selfish. You can't pour from an empty cup. You cannot keep giving when you haven't given yourself the time and care you need.

You deserve to have moments where the world can wait. Let others wait. Let them not understand why you're taking that time. Let them judge.

It's never a good idea to rush your self-care time, as it takes away from the true nourishment of the self-care. You deserve all the time and space needed. You deserve the necessity of slowing down, of turning off, of being *you*, without worrying about everyone else's needs.

It's not a crime to want peace. It's not a crime to take a break. It's necessary. It's vital. You're not a machine. You're a human who deserves rest and care.

You can stop apologizing for needing time for yourself. You can stop feeling like you have to explain why you're taking a break.

You deserve the right to choose when and how to recharge.

You deserve space to breathe, to think, to feel, to exist without the constant pressure of the world's demands. You don't need to wait for someone else to give you permission.

The only one who can give you permission is you. Give yourself that. Because you deserve it. Right now. And you deserve it every moment of every day that you decide you need it.

You Don't Have To Be Happy To Be Worthy

It's okay to not be happy all the time. It's okay to have those days where everything feels heavy, or you're just not in the best headspace. You don't need to be smiling every minute to be worthy of love, respect, or kindness.

Your sad self deserves love.

Your bland self deserves care.

Even your grumpy self deserves kindness.

Seriously.

You don't have to put on a happy face if it is not true. You don't need to protect others from your emotions. You are not here to play a character and hide the real you away. No one should hide themselves away.

You deserve to be seen for all of you, and be accepted for all of you. It may not seem like people can accept that, and the truth is, some people simply won't accept all of you.

Those people who expect you (and need you) to be happy all of the time are people who haven't been able to accept themselves for all of their emotional expressions. They lock those parts of them down, and when they see others express these parts, it scares them. It shows them something they are afraid to look at inside themselves, and so they try to shut that down in another person, too. Sometimes, you will be on the receiving end of someone dismissing your emotions.

But it doesn't make that okay. And it doesn't mean that you should also be treating yourself this way. It doesn't mean that you should lock down your feelings, too.

Take space from people who aren't able to hold your distress. Move away from relationships where you feel like all of you is not welcome.

Start designing connections where you know you can be accepted for all of who you are. It may take time to find these people, but they exist. Firstly, it starts with you accepting yourself for all parts of you.

You're allowed to feel whatever you feel. You don't have to pretend that everything's okay when it's not. You don't have to be "on" all the time. You're allowed to be low, to not have all the answers, to not have it all together.

That doesn't take away from your worth. You are still valuable. You are still worthy of love. Give yourself a lot of love when you aren't in the happiest space (it's when you need it most).

You don't need to have a perfect attitude or always be positive to be enough. Life doesn't work like that. You're human, and humans feel things. Sometimes, you're happy. Sometimes, you're not. And that's okay. Your worth is not defined by your mood, your energy, or your circumstances.

Happiness comes and goes. It's not something that's permanent, and it doesn't have to be. You don't need to be at your best to be deserving of care, attention, or anything else.

Take the pressure off. You don't have to be happy to be worthy.

You are enough just as you are, whether you're smiling or not.

Let Them Think Whatever They Think

Do you have a feeling that someone thinks something about you that doesn't feel nice or true?

You don't need to force yourself to be something that makes others feel comfortable. Whatever people think about you, let them.

You don't need to explain your choices, your life, or your reasons to anyone. People will have their opinions, and most of the time, they won't even know the full story. They will have many of their own stories, and they will filter your life through the lens they are wearing (the lens made up of their beliefs, experiences, prejudices, wounds, etc).

Let people think whatever they think. That is theirs, not yours.

You don't need to hold on to anyones judgments and take them as your own, even if they throw those judgments your way. You can decide to catch them and hold on, or let them go.

What if you just let people judge? Let them assume. Let them gossip. Let them hold their narrow views about who you should be or what you should do.

You're not here to meet their expectations.

You're not here to live a life that they think you should. Would that really make you happy?

Happiness is not found in making sure you mold someone else's thoughts to be a positive depiction of you. Happiness isn't found in making sure that people think of you in a certain way. It really isn't. Even if it feels that way right now.

You're here to live for yourself. You can make their opinions irrelevant to your peace. They can think whatever they want – and it can have nothing to do with you. Truly. It is 100% possible to free yourself from any impact that their thoughts, judgments, or words used to have on you.

You really can be someone who isn't touched by others opinions.

Sound's freeing, right?

You are allowed to stop trying to please people who aren't your people. You don't have to keep wasting your time and energy trying to make others understand or accept your choices. You're here to break free, to live in a way that's true to *you* – not to some imagined person that you're not.

People will always have something to say. That's the truth. People will eventually find fault with your way. Let them try to steer you another way. You don't need their approval, their permission, or their acceptance to keep doing what you're doing.

You don't have to follow any pathway they try to set for you. You're the only one who needs to approve of your life.

Remind yourself, when the judgments come: Let them think whatever they think. Keep being exactly who you are. It's your life, and you're living it on your own terms.

You Don't
Have To Fix
Everything

Did you unknowingly promote yourself as the fixer of the world without actually meaning to? Somehow stumble into a role that makes you feel like you're the only one able to handle all of the issues, yet you feel totally exhausted, overwhelmed, or burdened by it?

Despite how it feels, you really don't have to fix everything. You're not the only one has solutions. You don't have to make everything work perfectly. It's okay to stop carrying the weight of other people's lives.

Not everything needs to be fixed. Sometimes, things are messy, they're imperfect, and that's *okay*. Life doesn't need to be perfectly packaged to be worth living. And you aren't the only person out there to bring order to chaos.

Sometimes, order will be created by you, and that's lovely. Sometimes, order will be found from another's actions. And sometimes, there just won't be order. But there can still be peace.

You're not here to bear this burden alone. You don't need to come to the rescue every time something falls apart. You don't need to be the one who cleans up the chaos, smooths out the cracks, or makes everything *right* again.

Sometimes, letting things just *be* (even if they're not working) is exactly what's needed. You don't need to control everything or make it all look neat and tidy. Things can be broken and still be beautiful (and that includes you).

You're allowed to step back. You don't need to be involved in that situation. You don't need to take on that problem. And you don't need to have that conversation. You are allowed to step away from having to be the solution to everything.

The truth is, not every moment in life needs a fix. Not everything is a problem that needs solving. Not everything is yours to take on.

You're allowed to let go of that pressure, now.

So, will you let yourself let it go?

Maybe now is the time to let people make their own mistakes. Let situations unfold without you stepping in to save the day. It's *okay* to let other people carry their own load – sometimes, that is what is best for the person.

There's strength in knowing when to step back and say, "This isn't mine to fix."

Give yourself permission to let go. Stop thinking you need to fix it all. Life is messy, and it's beautiful. You don't need to fix the chaos to enjoy it. You don't need to be the hero every time something falls apart.

You are valuable, without being the solution. You are worthy, without being the "fixer."

You are enough, and you are safe, even as you let things be as they are.

You Are Not Behind

Measuring your progress against everyone else won't make you feel happy. It also won't help you progress.

If you're looking around and thinking you're falling behind because someone else is moving faster, doing more, or has their life more "together" than you, it's time to shift your focus because you are not behind.

You're exactly where you need to be. It sounds cheesy. But you are. How could you not be in the right place? There's no other right place than right now.

You may feel like you should be somewhere else. But in reality, everyone could always been somewhere else. This idea is one that will only make you feel that where you are is not enough. This thought is not helpful, productive, or of any use to you at all.

Time is not a race. You don't have to hit milestones according to some timeline or follow some imaginary schedule that society has handed you.

There is no "right" time for anything, no one-size-fits-all blueprint for how your life should unfold.

Your journey is *yours*, and it's not anyone else's business to decide how quickly or slowly it should go. This includes the part of you that is trying to tell yourself that you should be further along. You can let that part of you slowly, gently, become a little more quiet. How? By not feeding those thoughts. You don't need to wrestle with them, either. Just notice them and let them sit there in the background.

You don't have to rush. You don't have to play catch-up. You don't have to be anywhere other than where you are right now. Everyone's path looks different. And the fact that you're not at the same place as someone else doesn't mean you've failed. It just means you're moving at your own pace, and that's *perfectly fine*.

You're learning lessons, and you're moving along your own steps – those steps are perfect for you. It may not seem perfect, it may seem slow. Maybe it is slow. Can you simply let them be slow?

There's no age you're supposed to hit certain things by. There's no race to the finish line. Life isn't about speeding through to get to some destination. It's about experiencing it.

If someone else is ahead, great for them. It doesn't mean you're not behind. You can't be "behind" of your own life. Your life is playing out at the pace that is right for you.

Your time will come. Your path is unfolding.

You Don't Need To Justify Your Life Choices

You don't need to defend why you chose this job, this relationship, this path. Your choices are yours. They don't need to make sense to anyone else. People will always have opinions about what you should be doing, how you should be doing it, and when you should be doing it.

Let them. You don't have to explain yourself or get their approval.

You are the one walking this path. You know why you're doing what you're doing. And sometimes, you will know it is right but still not fully know why. The point is, you don't have to justify it with reasons that fit someone else's idea of what's "right."

You don't owe anyone your story, your process, or your reasons. You are allowed to live without needing to convince people that you're doing what's best for you.

You know the truth. You know why you are doing something. You understand. And that is enough.

Keep going. Trust yourself. Your choices are already valid, without any explanation at all. Even if someone tries to push for an explanation, you get to decide whether you give it.

Other people will have their stories and ideas about your choices. Whether they approve or not, it has nothing to do with you. Their opinions do not define you. Their expectations are not your responsibility.

You don't need to fit into their idea of who you should be or what your life should look like. You're not here to please anyone else.

You're here to live your truth, *unapologetically.*

Your life doesn't need permission, approval, or validation from anyone else. Your life just needs you to keep living it. You've got every right to make your own choices, even if they don't fit into someone else's view of success or happiness.

You don't need to justify your life choices. They're yours to make.

You Deserve
The Life You
Dream About

Not the one you've been told you're supposed to want. Not the life that fits into the mold someone else built for you. No, you deserve the life that makes your heart race, the one that feels like you're finally living *your* truth.

The one that inspires you to get out of bed every morning. The one that feels like home, even if no one else understands it.

Those dreams that you tell yourself are too farfetched? Those dreams you've been holding but not really allowing yourself to believe? They are possible. And you deserve that life.

The doubt is not yours, not really. That has been picked up by you somewhere along the way. Maybe someone else told you to doubt your dreams many years ago. Maybe the world has been subtly telling you that it can't happen.

But when you were a child, with unbound imagination, you tapped into the energy of possibility.

It truly did feel reachable. Not because you were a silly child. But because you didn't hold yourself back.

Now is the time to stop telling yourself that it's too big, too far out of reach, or that you're not worthy of it. You *are* worthy of everything you've ever dreamed of, even what feels impossible. Your dreams aren't some distant fantasy – they're your future in the making. If you let them be.

You don't have to shrink yourself to fit into a life that doesn't feel right. You don't have to downplay your dreams and goals to make them more acceptable for others to hear. Maybe others won't understand.

They might tell you that the dreams are not realistic. Let them think that. They can believe that, while you choose to believe something else.

You don't have to play small anymore. You don't have to keep sacrificing what you really want because it's easier to settle. You deserve the life that lights you up from the inside. You deserve the kind of joy that gives you the energy to keep creating a reality you've always wanted to be living.

Your dreams are not meant to be *optional*. They're not something to keep in the back of your mind or lock away because it feels "too risky" or "too big." You are worthy of the wildest, most unapologetic version of your life, and if you can see it, if you can dream it, then it's possible.

You might still have some reservations hearing these words. You might still feel hesitant. That's okay. Hesitation doesn't have to stop you. Insecurity doesn't have to be a barrier.

Confidence grows overtime, and little by little, one step at a time, as you keep moving towards your dreams, you'll start to believe more and more.

You deserve to wake up every single day and feel like you're exactly where you're meant to be, doing what makes you feel most *you*.

You deserve the life you dream about. You deserve it, and it's time to start living it.

You Are
Allowed To Be
Afraid

It's okay to feel scared and to be uncertain.

Whatever it is that you're afraid of; it's okay. You're safe. Even if it doesn't feel like it. It really is safe to be afraid.

Fear is not a weakness. It's not a sign that you're not capable. It doesn't mean you won't be able to move past these challenges. It doesn't mean that you will not make it through.

Even when it feels like you're facing something terrifying.

You're safe, right now, reading these words. And your fear is nothing to be ashamed of. Your fear is welcome. It doesn't make you weak.

Being afraid of things is a human experience, something everyone goes through. You don't have to pretend that everything's fine when it's not. You don't have to fake confidence or bravery. You're allowed to feel afraid – and still move forward anyway.

The irony is, letting yourself feel fear is actually courageous.

Fear doesn't mean you're not strong. It doesn't mean that you won't be strong in the future. It doesn't mean you're not worthy of success. It means you're facing a challenge.

You might be pushing yourself to something new, to something outside your comfort zone. Or maybe you're dealing with a difficult situation that has you wondering how you'll make it through. Whatever that edge is, know that your fear can be proof that you're growing, that you're stepping into uncharted territory, and that you're allowing yourself to build resilience.

You don't need to shut the fear down. You don't need to run from it. And you definitely don't need to be ashamed of it. You can rightfully be afraid, without any shame.

You're doing wonderfully.

You're allowed to be afraid, and still take that next step. You're allowed to feel that knot in your stomach and still choose to face whatever is ahead.

Being afraid doesn't stop you from being powerful. It doesn't stop you from being capable. It doesn't stop you from moving toward what you want. It's just a feeling.

And you don't have to let it control you.

If you feel you need to rest, take rest. If you think it's time to ask for support, then ask. Your fear doesn't have to be faced alone.

You don't have to beat it. You just need to let yourself feel it, support yourself in whatever way you can, and keep moving at any pace, anyway. Fear doesn't define you. You define you.

You are allowed to be afraid.

It's Okay If You Want To Hide

Sometimes, you just need to disappear for a little while.

You don't have to keep showing up for everyone, playing the role, being the person they expect, or being the person you expect yourself to be. You don't have to be out there all the time. It's okay to slip away for a bit. To hide out. To get quiet. To not reply to everyone and to not update the world on what is happening.

You don't have to keep putting on a brave face or pretending like you've got it all together. You don't have to force yourself to show up with energy when you have absolutely none left.

You don't need to explain why you're pulling away, and you don't need anyone's permission to do it.

You're allowed to take a break from all the things, even if they're things you love. It doesn't mean you're weak for wanting to hide. It doesn't mean you're failing. It just means you're human. And humans need to step back.

We're not meant to give and give and show up with boundless energy all the time. That's a big expectation to place on yourself.

We're not meant to perform, to keep pushing, and to always be available – even to the people we care about. If you need to hide, to retreat, to just exist without the constant expectation to engage, that is so okay. Give yourself that.

It doesn't make you any less of who you are. It doesn't make you any less worthy of love, connection, or success. You have nothing to prove. Hiding doesn't take away from all that you deserve in life.

You don't have to explain it, you don't have to apologize for it. If the world feels too big, too loud, too demanding, or just simply a little too much right now, take a step back. You're allowed to disappear for as long as you need.

You don't even have to understand exactly why you feel the strong need to hide. You can want to hide and just give yourself that without having to work out where it is coming from. Maybe you find out later. Maybe not, The point is, you have every right to hide.

Whatever the reason is, you're allowed to escape. Take the space to heal, to rest, to do absolutely nothing, and to come back to yourself.

When you're ready, trust that you'll emerge stronger, clearer, and more aligned with who you really are and what you really want.

It really is okay if you want to hide. Sometimes, that's the best thing you can do.

Change Your Mind As Many Times As You Need

You don't owe anyone a consistent story. You don't have to stay loyal to an idea or decision simply because you once wanted that. It's okay if you change your mind. And if that happens again and again.

Let them tell you that you are being confusing. Let people say whatever they want to say. They are not living your life. You are.

And what matters is the story that you tell yourself. Are you telling yourself that you're not allowed to change your mind? Are you feeling locked into something because changing your mind means something negative about you?

Let yourself change your mind as many times as you need. There will also be people in your life who are very supportive of this for you. They might see that a change is needed, for the sake of your health or happiness.

If you feel a change is needed, then let yourself make the change.

You don't have to stay on the same path just because you started it. You're allowed to change your direction, to pivot, to completely rework your plans.

You are not bound by the choices you made in the past.

Life is fluid, and you get to evolve with it. Every moment of every day.

So many of us hold onto decisions we've made – things we said we would do or places we said we would go – because we're scared to change our minds. We think it's too late, or we think we'll disappoint someone. But there is nothing wrong with changing your mind.

It's not a sign of weakness. It's a sign of growth. It means you're paying attention, that you're listening to yourself, and that you're allowing yourself to evolve.

Changing your mind isn't failure. It's wisdom. It's clarity. It's knowing that where you were headed doesn't align with where you are now. That's not a mistake. That's called *living,* learning, growing, and adjusting. If something doesn't fit, change it. If something doesn't feel right, let it go.

You are allowed to reassess, to hit the reset button, and to decide that you want something else. You don't need anyone's permission to change direction. You don't need to justify your choices to anyone.

Your life is yours to design, and if you need to change your mind a thousand times, do it. You are not obligated to stick with what no longer serves you.

Change your mind as many times as you need, and trust that every change is leading you closer to the version of yourself you're becoming.

You're Allowed
To Put
Yourself First

It's not selfish to put yourself first.

Do you feel guilty for wanting to choose yourself? You're not alone. Most of us have been led to believe that putting ourselves first is not kind, not selfless, and not acceptable.

We think that to be a good person that makes people like us and feel comfortable around us, we have to always put everyone else before us.

But where does that really leave you? Do you feel energized at the end of the day of putting everyone else's needs before yours? Often, we keep this up for some time until we can't any longer.

Until we are depleted, resentful, and wishing that someone would just take care of us.

Here's some tough love for you: **you need to take care of you.**

Your resentment isn't even towards them, it's towards you. For not putting yourself first. If you're taking care of everyone BUT you, you are neglecting yourself. And if you see yourself as a kind and loving person – what about that kindness and love for you?

Let yourself choose yourself. Make your needs a priority. You already know that filling yourself up will help you show up for others with more energy and patience.

You don't have to keep putting everyone else ahead of you while you run on empty. Your time, your energy, your well-being – they matter just as much as anyone else's.

And you deserve to take care of them so that you can show up in life how you truly want to show up – with grounded, balanced energy.

You don't need to apologize for needing space. You don't need to explain why you need a break, why you need time to recharge, why you need to say no, and why you are changing your mind.

You don't owe anyone your last drop of energy. It's okay to do something that is for no one else but for you. You don't have to feel like you're letting people down just because you're not available every second.

Putting yourself first doesn't mean you don't care about others. It means you care enough about yourself to show up fully when you're needed. If you're drained, if you're burned out, if you've given everything, there's nothing left for anyone else.

You can't give to others what you don't give to yourself first.

You are allowed to prioritize your mental health, your happiness, and your peace. You don't need to be everyone's everything.

You don't need to take on everyone's burdens or solve everyone's problems. You are allowed to focus on your own path, your own growth, your own needs, without guilt.

You're allowed to put yourself first. You are worthy of your own time, your own care, your own attention.

And that's not just okay – it's necessary. What would putting yourself first look like right now?

You Are
Lovable

Even when you're messy. You are lovable.

Even when you are being a bit difficult (or a lot difficult), you are lovable.

Even for all of the mistakes you have made, including hurting others. You are no less deserving of love. When you're not feeling like yourself, you are still worthy of love. When you think you're too much or not enough, you deserving of love.

You don't need to be perfect to be loved. You don't need to have it all figured out for people to love you. You don't need to act a certain way or fit into some mold to deserve love.

If anyone makes you feel like you have to change to be loved, that's not your problem. You don't need to let that in your life. You are lovable and never need to prove it. No extra effort needed.

You are lovable just by being you. Exactly as you are, with all your quirks, flaws, difficulties, wounds, and moments of doubt.

You don't need to do something extra to earn love. You don't need to hide parts of yourself and show up how you think they want you to. You don't need to shape shift, take something away, add something more, and make any additional adjustments to be lovable.

You're allowed to be raw. You don't need to be shiny and perfect to be worthy of affection, attention, or care. Every single part of you is lovable.

Love doesn't work that way. It's not a prize you have to win. It's not a badge you have to earn. You're worthy of love *now*. Just the way you are. Not because of anything. But just because.

It's Okay If They Don't Understand

Feel like they just don't understand?

Like no matter what you say and how you explain yourself, they just don't get it? It's hard to feel misunderstood.

Although it feels like it right now, you don't need to make everyone else see things your way. You don't have to explain yourself to make others "get it." That isn't the only pathway to you feeling at peace. Even if it feels like it.

You don't need to justify why you do what you do or feel how you feel to get them to understand and approve. It's okay to trust yourself and to stand firm in your own truth – even if it doesn't fit neatly into someone else's expectations.

You don't need to carry someone else's confusion about your life as if it's your responsibility to fix that for them.

You don't need to bend, twist, or shape yourself to fit someone else's idea of who you should be or to make them feel clear about why you're making your choices.

Your choices are yours, and they don't have to fit into a mold that feels safe or familiar to others. Your life is yours to live, and you are allowed to take steps that make sense for you – even if no one else can understand why. Ultimately, it's not theirs to understand.

What matters is that you understand yourself. You trust your own intuition, your own desires, your choices, your beliefs, and your own growth.

You can move forward without someone's validation and approval. You really can. You're also allowed to feel sad for not being understood. Both can exist; the sadness at being misunderstood and the acceptance that it is okay if they don't get it.

What matters is that you own your choices. That you trust that you guided the way you are guided for a reason (and sometimes, even you won't understand it).

What matters is that you're staying true to yourself.

You are allowed to live your truth without waiting for the world to understand it. They don't have to get it. But you? You get to keep going, no matter what.

It's Okay
To Let Go
Of Long-Term
Relationships

It's hard to let go of someone when they have been in your life for years. You've shared memories, experiences, or even deep emotional connection.

There is a lot of history there, so letting go of these relationships can be extremely difficult to do. You might feel loyal to the connection, even if it is not giving you the same joy or value as it might have used to.

Although you feel this tug of history pull you to stay, it doesn't mean you have to hold onto them forever.

People change, including you. And sometimes, the relationships that once fit and that once made sense no longer do. That's okay. You're allowed to walk away, even if it is hard. Walking away is walking towards something that is more aligned and nourishing for you, and that is always a good idea.

Maybe it's a peaceful ending, where you both let go gently. Maybe it's a more complicated ending that leaves you feeling sad. Endings happen in all manner of ways, and you'll never really know how it will be until it happens.

You can try to create a peaceful ending, but the truth is, it's not just up to you. If another person (or more) is involved, it will also be up to them how to navigate this.

Letting go of a long-term relationship will bring grief with it. It doesn't matter how right the decision is; you've shared so much, and that will leave an imprint. You will miss many things.

You will be processing that for some time. That still doesn't mean it is the wrong choice.

Sometimes the right choice feels wrong at first.

You don't have to feel guilty for knowing that a relationship is not right anymore. You don't have to force a connection that doesn't feel valuable to continue devoting your energy to anymore. Holding onto a relationship for the sake of history; for the sake of avoiding the discomfort of change, doesn't serve you or them.

You'll know if you're holding on for reasons that are not serving your highest good. And that is something important to listen to.

Sometimes, the most loving thing you can do - for yourself and for the other person - is to let go.

They may see it this way, too. Or they may not be able to understand this.

Letting go doesn't mean you're erasing the past. It doesn't mean you didn't care and that you don't still care. It just means you're making space for what's next. It means you're creating room for healthier, more aligned connections. It means you're allowing yourself to evolve, even if it means parting ways with people who can't grow with you.

It's okay to acknowledge that a relationship has run its course. It doesn't make you a bad person. It doesn't make them a bad person. It doesn't discount the beautiful times you had. None of it was a waste.

Letting go means that you're brave enough to make the choices that serve your best self. You deserve relationships that lift you up, that nurture you, and that allow you to thrive. If someone no longer adds that to your life, and you have tried and persisted and it still hasn't changed, it really is okay to let go. No matter what anyone else says.

You're not abandoning anyone. You're honoring yourself. And continuing to stay would be abandoning yourself. You're respecting someone else to not hold on to what isn't feeling aligned for you anymore. That's the most loving thing you can do.

You Are More Than Your Achievements

You are not defined by what you've accomplished. Your worth is not in by the titles you hold, the money you make, or the awards you've received. Your value is not in how well you have succeeded.

It may feel like it right now, but that's not where your true value comes from. Your worth is intrinsic. It was there the moment you were born (actually, before that, if we're being honest).

You don't have to keep proving yourself to feel worthy. You don't need to list off all of your accolades in order to convince people of your place in the world.

You don't have to keep climbing, striving, and achieving, just to feel validated. You are so much more than what you achieve.

Let's consider what it took for you to get here on this earth; of all the potential life that could have been, and that was not given the chance to materialize earth-side – *you did.*

You somehow beat the odds of surviving what it takes for life to be initiated and to form inside of your mother, and for you to be here reading these words now. **You are a miracle.**

You are an incredibly magical being. In all of your ordinary-ness – you are magical. The fact that you are here is magical. The fact that you have formed an independent character of who you are; one that keeps growing and learning and showing up.

That is nothing short of a miracle. It's just that we are so used to existing that we forget how miraculous it is.

Your worth doesn't increase with every milestone you hit, and it doesn't decrease when you take a break. It doesn't fluctuate the way that life fluctuates. It truly doesn't. It will always be there, no matter how you feel, what you've done, or anything else that you are worried might make you be "less than."

You can't be "less than" who you are, and who you are is whole and enough. It doesn't matter whether you've hit every goal or whether you're still figuring it out.

Your achievements are *part* of your story, but they don't impact how valuable you are. Sure, people might try to push this narrative, and the media certainly will attempt to convince you that your value is dependent on your looks, achievements, financial status, relationship status, or any other indicator of superiority that is relevant to your culture.

But at the end of the day, it's all a story.

You get to choose if you tell yourself this story, too.

Those things don't define who you are, what you're capable of, or how much love and compassion you carry inside. They definitely have nothing to do with how lovable you are. You are not just what you've done and what you will do. You are all of you – your growth, your struggles, your moments of challenge, your wounds, your messiness, your laughter, your vulnerability, your wisdom.

You are *whole*. The achievements will come and go, but your value? It stays. You are more than what you've achieved.

It's Safe To Let Go Of Control

I know it feels like you have to hold everything together, like if you don't keep a tight grip on every little thing, it will fall apart.

Maybe you've been feeling this way for a long time. Maybe all of your life, to some degree.

And you know what? Maybe it is true that you were the only one to be able to take care of things.

It could be true that once upon a time, without you, some things wouldn't have worked out. Letting go of control doesn't mean to discount that you have done (and can do) powerful things.

You have solutions and ideas and answers and plans that work, and that's wonderful.

But here's the truth: you don't need to control everything (and everyone) to feel safe. You don't need to manage every outcome, every situation, or every moment.

If you've been doing it for a very long time, it becomes the normal thing to do, without even thinking about it anymore. It became a protective shield for you. It most likely did protect you in many situations, too. Let's not discount that. But it has also become a pattern that doesn't always help you (even if the voice inside says you have to control to feel safe, still).

Right now, it's okay to release the weight you're carrying. It's okay to trust that things can unfold without your constant intervention.

It's okay to let go of control. I know it feels hard. That's normal. It's okay that it's hard. It doesn't make it any less true that you will be okay.

You can rest.

You've been holding on so tightly for so long because it feels like control is the only thing keeping you afloat, like if you let go for even a second, the whole world will crash down. That no one would be there to catch you. That may have been true once. But it doesn't mean that it is still true.

You *can* let go. You *are* safe. The fear that's telling you otherwise? It's just fear. It's the fear that keeps you in fight-or-flight mode, believing that if you don't have control you're at risk. That you might not survive. Rationally, you know you'll survive. But your body is likely still not understanding this.

It might take a little time for your body to learn that you can safely let go. You can go slow. Let the body catch up to what you know is true, deep down.

It's okay to trust the process. It's okay to trust others. It's okay to trust yourself – to trust that even when you can't control everything, you'll still be okay. It's not about trusting yourself to keep controlling.

It's about trusting yourself that you don't need to control any longer.

Life is unpredictable, and yes, it's scary sometimes, and yes, you'll need to step up, but you don't have to face it gripping onto control constantly. When you let go, trust that you can handle whatever comes.

Letting go doesn't actually mean you lose anything. When you let go of control, you create space for peace. When you let go, you have space to pick up something else.

When you let go of control, you give yourself room to breathe, to feel, and to simply exist without the constant pressure of perfection pushing down on you. You allow things to happen without forcing them into place.

In that space you can find real strength. The kind of strength that doesn't come from micromanaging every part of your life, but from knowing that you are capable of handling life's flow, even when it doesn't look how you expected. You give yourself room to feel, think, and to even find solutions organically without forcing them.

It's safe to let go of control. You don't have to do everything yourself. You don't have to hold onto the reins so tightly anymore.

It's okay to trust that you're safe, that things will work out, and that even when you don't have all the answers, you can let life unfold. Let people be as they are. Let life reveal its answers to you.

See what magic may happen when you let go.

You Can Feel Peaceful Inside Yourself

It doesn't matter how chaotic the world gets, how loud the noise is around you, or how messy things might seem.

If things outside of you are difficult right now, you *can* find peace within you. If people are creating some conflict and resistance, you can still touch that place of deep peace within yourself.

You don't need to wait for everything to align perfectly and for the storm to pass for you to feel better.

There is a calmness within you, beyond all of the movement. That peace is there right now, just buried under layers of disregulation. Pause for a moment as you're reading these words – close your eyes and see if you can touch it; this stillness inside.

If you've been waiting for someone else to make you feel calm, as if they're the only ones who can create that for you, remember that peace isn't something that *happens to you* – it's something *you create* inside yourself.

People may support with that process, but they aren't the ones to create it. Ultimately, it's a choice that you make (even when it feels like it's too hard).

It's okay to choose peace. You don't have to let every moment of chaos pull you into its current. You are allowed to take a step back, breathe deeply, and find your center.

You get to claim your right to protect your peace in whatever way feels right for you. Maybe that is taking time away from your regular routine. Maybe that is telling people no. Maybe that is taking better care of your mental health by setting boundaries with yourself. Or it could even be getting help from the outside so you can feel more resourced to create your peace and maintain it.

The world will keep spinning but you can choose to be still. You don't have to get pulled into noise, the rush, or the drama. You can tune it out and turn inward.

You're allowed to turn away from things to find your peace. It doesn't make you selfish. It doesn't make you "dismissive" – it makes you mindful and caring of yourself. It is a radical act of self love (even if others don't understand it).

You truly do have all you need within yourself to feel peaceful inside. Perhaps you're just out of practice? Maybe now is the time to start that practice of connecting to the peace within you.

Peace isn't about avoiding discomfort. It's about knowing that even in the midst of it you can find stillness inside.

Peace is already within you, waiting to be acknowledged and to be nurtured.

When you give yourself permission to be still, to sit with your breath, and to listen to the quiet spaces in between, that's when you discover the peace that was always there.

It's Okay To Have Doubt

Not sure what to do? Feeling uncertain right now? It's not the most comfortable feeling, to sit with doubt.

But doubt isn't the enemy. It's not something to be afraid of. It's not something that should force you into action, when you aren't ready.

It's not something that you have to fix or solve, just so you can stop feeling the discomfort of doubt.

You're allowed to doubt things. You can doubt people, situations, and yourself. It doesn't make you bad, wrong, or untrusting. It makes you human.

Maybe your doubt is based on reality, and there are many strong reasons for the doubt to be there. Maybe the doubt is coming from old insecurities and memories of the past.

Yes, doubt can feel like it is getting in the way of things. Of course, you want it to go. But forcing it away, denying it, and trying to rush a solution and force clarity isn't a helpful way forward.

What can help in moments of doubt is to simply let it be there. It's okay that you have doubt. You're not weak for doubting. And you don't have to be afraid that it is always going to be there, either. Clarity will come. It always does.

Maybe right now the doubt is exactly where you need to be.

Maybe it is there because the answers aren't yet ready to be revealed. Maybe this in-between space of not knowing is giving you something else valuable that you can't yet feel or see. Maybe you can relax into the doubt, accept it as it is, and get curious about it.

Work with the doubt rather than push it away. Ask it why it might be there. What is it trying to tell you? It might have a message for you. Or it might simply be offering you the perfect moment to pause and rest.

We all have doubt.

There's nothing wrong with you for feeling it. Let it be as it is. It's okay.

It's Okay To Walk Away From What Drains You

What is exhausting you? What is making you feel utterly drained of energy and life? There are things in our lives that we can't exactly walk away from. Responsibilities are very real. But then there are things (and people) that we can walk away from. It may be hard to do that, but it doesn't mean that we can't.

You deserve to walk towards what gives you energy, makes you feel radiant, and renews your spirit.

You don't have to endure what drains you out of obligation or loyalty to something that you know is not going to get better. If it has been draining you for a while (or even for a little), then it is time to prioritize yourself.

If you have the freedom to walk away, that is yours to take.

It doesn't make you "inconsistent", or "non-committal" to walk away. Sure, they are potential narratives you could tell yourself, or let others tell you, but you get to choose the story you hold onto.

Why not make it a story of victory? Why not let your walking away be a celebration of your boundaries?

Give yourself some softness.

Forgive yourself if you aren't following through with something.

Know that by walking away from what drains you, you are walking towards what energizes you and that is a wonderful thing. That is a powerful and beautiful act of kindness to yourself. And that means something. That will make you feel cared for, supported, and loved – all from yourself. What a powerful thing.

No one else can walk away from something for you. No one else can give you permission. You might be trying to seek that permission from someone else. That's understandable. But know that you are the only one who can really give yourself permission.

You deserve to be energized by what you do. You deserve to choose what you devote your energy to, and design your life in line with what makes you feel lit up.

There may be things you can't change, but there is a lot that you can. And what drains you might not even be anything external.

Maybe it is something you've been carrying inside... A thought pattern, a belief, a habit, or a way that you talk to yourself. The same goes here, too. It's okay to walk away from anything internally that drains you.

Claim a life that gives you energy.

You deserve it, and it is possible. Let it be yours. Only you can allow that, by deciding what you let in, and what you walk away from.

You Don't Have to Be Strong All the Time

Does it seem like the world worships strength? That you're expected to hold it together no matter what?

You're not the only one who has been sold this narrative.

The thing is, you're not a robot. You're allowed to feel weak, to be vulnerable, and to let the cracks show. You don't have to have it all figured out, or have all the answers, or keep going when you're running on empty.

You certainly don't have to put on a brave face to be accepted, or to "stay strong" like so many "inspirational" memes are trying to tell us.

Sometimes, being strong means knowing when to stop. Most of us didn't learn this when we were learning about life as young little beings navigating the world.

We learned that we had to be tough and that for others to praise us, we couldn't let our weakness show.

In many cases, we did have to be tough in hard situations, and stay strong in order to survive. That is true, too, and let's not brush aside that truth. You were strong when you needed to be, and you can be strong again.

But it is also a strength to own your limitations and to know when you can and when you can't do something. It's a strength to admit it, accept it, and to let yourself be seen in your vulnerability.

It's incredibly strong to show the sides of you that you think are "weak."

It's okay to admit that you're not okay. You're allowed to take a breath, to take a break, to ask for help. Needing a moment (or more) to collapse doesn't make you weak.

It makes you human. And it shows a deep humility, courage, rawness, and realness. That is a strength.

Trying to be strong all of the time is ironically the thing that weakens us; because we don't listen to our bodies and minds when they tell us that we need a break, or when they make their boundaries clear.

Real strength is knowing when to rest, when to step back, and when to put your needs first. The world might try to tell you that you have to be tough, that you have to push through everything, but that's not where your true strength is built. Strength doesn't mean being untouchable.

Strength means being *real and* being honest with yourself about what you need. Strength is giving yourself permission to take a step back when you need it.

It's funny that by realizing you don't have to be strong all the time, you are showing strength.

You can let go of the pressure to be unbreakable. You're allowed to be tired. You're allowed to rest. You don't have to be strong all the time to be worthy, to be enough, to be loved.

You are allowed to exist as you are, right now.

It's Okay If You Feel Like Being Silent

You are one hundred million percent allowed to have no desire at all to say anything to anyone. Nope. Nothing. You don't owe anyone words. It's not a requirement for you to be valuable, worthy, or a good person.

If you feel like keeping quiet, and protecting your peace by sitting in silence for a while, then let yourself have that. For as long as you need.

Hide away, and be silent.

Let people call you anti-social. Let yourself be on the outside. Whether you're introverted, or just plain sick of speaking to people, it's more than okay to be silent.

If you feel like just being in your own company, enjoy that.

You're allowed to withdraw. You can absolutely choose to be left alone and disconnect from people and the world.

You don't have to show up when you're not feeling able to. You don't have to say words that you don't mean.

You don't have to pretend that you're outgoing and social and engaged when you really don't feel that way. Honor how you feel. Honor what is true for you.

You deserve to let yourself show up however you want to.

Don't make an effort, if you don't feel able or ready to. Feel tired of people-ing? Then stop people-ling. Feel sick of socializing? Then hermit yourself away. Wrap yourself up in your blanket like a burrito, if that's what you feel like doing. You get that. You are so allowed to feel this way.

Whatever you have to do or say to claim that space to be in your own company, your own thoughts, and your silence, then let yourself do that. You really are allowed to not want to speak to anyone.

It doesn't make you anti-social or too shy or introverted or anything else. It's just the reality of how you feel. Why would you expect anything else from yourself than being truthful and real?

Everything else is a compromise on your needs and wants. Which will never feel good. It'll only fracture your relationship with yourself and have you show up inauthentic. No one really wants that, anyway.

So, trust that if you don't want to speak to anyone, that it's not a bad thing at all. It doesn't make you a bad person. It doesn't make you unkind. It makes you real, and by honoring your boundaries, it makes you respectful to yourself. That is a great thing!

Your desire to connect and interact will come back again, eventually. You can trust that you'll decide to engage in the way that feels best for you, whenever that is. But you don't need it to be there right now.

You don't need to feel bad about just wanting to keep to yourself. Let yourself have that. It is your birthright. Enjoy it. Soak up that delicious silence.

You Don't Need To Hold On Anymore

You've carried it for long enough, haven't you? The pain. The weight. The regret. The person. The old dreams. Those outdated ways of being. The fear. The control. The sadness. The victim-state. The memories that keep you awake at night....

You don't have to clutch onto all of that, holding it close like it's part of you. It's not. **You are not it**. And if it were part of your identity in the past, you are not that person anymore. You are ready to let go now.

It's time to let it go now.

You're allowed to put it down. You're allowed to stop dragging it around like a suitcase full of things you no longer need. You don't need to hold onto that anger, that hurt, or that fear anymore. It's not yours to carry. It never was.

Whatever it might have been giving you – validation, approval, love, connection, satisfaction, protection and safety... It has served its purpose, but you don't need it moving forward.

You have other ways to feel all the things you wish to feel. You have more resources now. And you will keep getting more healthy resources to help yourself stay safe and feel connected. Trust that this is the direction of your life.

It will be hard to heal while you're still gripping tightly onto those things. You can't move forward when you're still living in the past. You don't have to keep holding onto the *what-ifs* or the *should-haves.*

They're not helping you grow. They're not helping you move through the world with an open heart. It's okay to let go, now. For you to feel the peace that you're really looking for and to let the healing truly happen, it's time to stop holding on.

Letting go doesn't mean you're forgetting or giving up. It doesn't mean you don't honor the past for what is was. It doesn't mean you're being disrespectful.

It means you're choosing to make space for new things, for peace, for growth, for a version of you that's not weighed down by things you can't change.

You're allowed to release the grip, to breathe freely, to let the past stay in the past, and to finally move forward.

It really is as simple as that: to let it go. It's not about throwing it away, forcing it down, or pushing it strongly out of your life. When you are not holding on anymore, it requires little effort, like opening your hand and letting it slip out of your fingers. Letting go simply means you're just not holding on anymore.

You know the relief of opening that tightly held hand that was holding onto something physically heavy? That feeling of setting it down and feeling the hand lighten and release... That is the relief that is waiting for you.

That is truly what it feels like; to set a heavy thing down is embracing the delicious rest that you get to have.

The truth is, it takes a lot of energy to grip tightly. It has been taking a lot of energy from you to hold on. Especially if you've been carrying this for a long time. Imagine where that energy could be going instead. Imagine how much more space you would have within yourself for something else entirely. Something good for you. Something healing, positive, and growth-filled.

That's what is waiting for you when you let go.

You don't need to hold on anymore. You can be free, right now. If you make that choice. It's yours to make.

You don't need to hold on anymore.

You Deserve
Respect

Not because you've earned it or because you've jumped through anyone's hoops.

Not because you have reached some level of success.

Not because you are a level higher than everyone else.

Not because you've hustled yourself so hard that you're ready to hit the ground.

You deserve respect simply because you *exist*. Because you are human. Because you are worthy. Full stop.

You don't need to prove your worth to anyone in order to gain respect. You don't need to bend over backward to get someone's approval. Respect isn't something you should have to beg for, and it isn't something you should have to *earn* through meeting someone else's expectations.

You deserve to have your boundaries respected. You deserve to have your opinion respected. You deserve to have your time respected. You deserve to have your thoughts respected.

You deserve to be treated with kindness, dignity, and consideration. And if someone can't give that to you? They are not the people for you. You don't need to tolerate disrespect from anyone – family, friends, coworkers, strangers, and yourself.

You deserve to be seen and heard, not dismissed or belittled. If someone can't treat you the way you deserve, walk away.

And if you are not respecting yourself, it's time to change that. It's time to show up for yourself with the respect you crave from others.

Respect isn't optional. It's a baseline. You are worthy of being treated with decency, no matter who you are, what you've been through, what you've done, or what others think of you. If someone is not respecting you, it is a moment for you to respect yourself enough to move away from that.

Self respect means not allowing people's disrespect.

You deserve respect – and you are worthy of it. Your feelings, your voice, and your presence matter. You matter. It's time to start treating yourself that way.

You Are
Allowed To
Outgrow People

People change. You change. That is inevitable.

You will outgrow people and it is not a bad thing at all.

It's not a reflection of their worth or yours. It's not a
failure when relationships end. It's a very natural part
of life. As you evolve, your values, priorities, and desires
change, too. That's not only okay, it's great.

Not everyone you encounter will be meant to stay in your
life forever, and letting these relationships shift is a very
respectful thing to do.

In fact, if your relationships always stayed the same
throughout your entire life it is likely because you are
not on the path led by growth, but instead, trying to stay
the same and perhaps stuck in old ways of being.

Hanging on to things that aren't serving you anymore, including people, will only keep you stationary as your body, heart, and mind try to move you forward naturally. You'll be keeping yourself stuck, resisting the organic flow of life.

Not all relationships are outgrown. Some stay, because they grow as you do. Some relationships will shift and evolve and feel different from how they used to, but are still valuable and still enrich your life (or even bring greater fulfillment as they change).

Then, there are some that just don't feel aligned anymore. They aren't giving you the fulfillment and nourishment that you deserve and they don't feel quite "right" to continue to devote your energy to.

It is not running away – it is simply you moving towards what you know is best for you. You're not abandoning anyone or betraying someone by outgrowing people. It is just a simple fact of life.

Sometimes, it's easy as both people feel the same. Sometimes, it's hard, and there will be a challenge.

You know if it is running away and avoiding, or if it is simply outgrowing that is happening.

Trust yourself that you understand what is best for you. Is it the evolved you now (the new version of yourself) that is holding on to the person, or is it the past version of you that you have outgrown that is holding on out of fear?

It can be a difficult process to let go, and you might feel like if you outgrow them you won't find another relationship that is aligned and as valuable as this one used to be.

But the truth is, by letting go of what is not right, you are making more space to be able to call in that relationship that is aligned.

Stepping away is actually the most respectful and peaceful thing you can do. It's not about abandoning people; it's about acknowledging that the path you're on might no longer align with the path they're on. It's about honoring your growth, which is an important and powerful thing to do.

Tap into the peace and clarity that you know is true. Lead yourself towards a more crystal clear, connected, and rich life that has fulfilling relationships that match your growth.

Again – some people grow with you, alongside you, and your relationship gets deeper, more colorful, and more precious. Some people grow in different directions. Both are perfect. Both are natural. Both deserve to be respected.

You are allowed to outgrow people. And it's not only okay – it's necessary for your life to continue to flourish.

You're doing the right thing.

Even if it feels hard. Trust yourself.

You Are Doing Better Than You Think

You really are.

Stop for a second and just take stock of the stories you've been telling yourself about your progress. Whether it is your inner-growth, your outward success, your physical body or emotional regulation, your money-making ability or your mental capacity, how capable you feel of doing hard things, or how peaceful you feel inside of yourself...

Do you have a story that you aren't doing as well as you want to be? That you aren't "there yet" and that you "should be" there already?

It's easy to get caught up in what you haven't done yet, in what's still on your to-do list, in where you'd rather be, and the progress you'd rather have.

That's a very natural place to be. Not a helpful place or one that will bring you peace, but it is normal to feel this way.

But just because you feel that way doesn't mean that it's true. And it doesn't mean you have to keep feeling that way.

It might feel true, especially if you've been telling yourself these stories for a long time (like most people). But again, just because you tell yourself this, and just because it *feels true*, still doesn't mean it is true.

You are doing far better than you think. The only thing stopping you from seeing that is the attachment to the idea that you're not doing good.

Here's the thing: You're showing up, even when you don't want to. You're trying, even if it is only a little bit. You're moving forward, even when it feels like you're stuck. That is worth celebrating. Every tiny win is worth celebrating. Putting yourself down because the win wasn't big enough is not helping you.

Forgive yourself if you've been doing that. It's okay. And forgive yourself if you've been believing that you aren't doing as well as you want to be. Those stories? They don't make you bad. Let's not get caught up in feeling bad about feeling bad. That's a silly trap.

If you haven't yet been able to see that you're doing better than you think, that's okay. Forgive yourself for being hard on yourself and having high standards and expectations. Now, reroute how you think. It's very possible to reroute your thoughts. You definitely have the power to do that.

If you're thinking right now, "but that's hard!" Yes, you're right. It is. But you've done hard things. You've done many many many hard things, so you can absolutely do this. You can shift how you feel about yourself.

Change the story. You really are doing better than you think. Give yourself props for the growth you've experienced. Every step you've taken, no matter how small, has moved you closer to where you want to be.

You can stop being so hard on yourself, now. That hardness never actually helped you. It never moved you more forward in your growth. It's just a pattern you learned to do long ago when you tried to "be better" for people around you.

You learned to be hard on yourself because people were hard on you. But how they treated you wasn't helpful either. Maybe it stopped you from "playing up" and "making mistakes", but did it help you actually grow in a good direction, led by inner peace, balance, and wisdom? Nope.

So, you can stop treating yourself that way, too. You don't need to be hard on yourself to do better. You don't need to have strict and strong standards of self blame and a "not-good-enough-yet" mentality in order for you to move forward.

You get let go of that now and use that energy to keep moving forward with kindness and support.

You are doing better than you give yourself credit for. And sometimes, the biggest achievement is just showing up and trying your best.

Give yourself kindness, especially when you're going slow, making mistakes, and taking more time than you would like yourself to take.

Keep supporting yourself. Keep showing up, and be soft and kind to yourself as you do.

You're doing better than you think and it's time for you to
see that.

It's Okay To Do Nothing

Yep.

Nothing at all.

Nada. Zilch.

Nothing. No errands. No tasks. No words. No productivity. No things to check off on your to-do list. No showing up where you normally would. No putting yourself out there.

If you have an urge to do nothing right now – take no action, make no decision, and let life and yourself be as you are. Give yourself that. It's okay to do nothing. You don't always have to be doing something in order to feel worthy and valuable. Doing all the things isn't alway the right thing to do. Sometimes, nothing is exactly what is needed.

Let go.

Do nothing. Nothing at all.

Empty.

You are allowed to stop trying to solve, fix, and think your way through things. You can stop trying to do all the things you want to. Sure, there are many things you want and need to do, and there's time for that later. Right now, nothing feels right, so let yourself rest in that space of nothing.

Nowhere to go. Nowhere to be. Nothing to say. Nothing to think. Nothing to solve. Nothing to do.

The simple, beautiful, spacious realm of nothingness is where some of the greatest beauty is found. But don't do it in search of the beauty. That's the trick. Because that is still "doing something", right? Sneaky how we catch ourselves thinking that we are in nothingness but we are still there to "get something" from it.

If there is anything to "get" from nothingness, it is the peace of nothingness. But the irony is, if you are chasing the peace, you're still not led by nothingness.

Here's how you can really let yourself do nothing:

Release all expectation of what you'll get from doing nothing. Release all pressure for how you should be in nothingness. Release any idea of what you will think and feel when you drop everything else.

Just do nothing. Sit there. Give yourself space. No need to work those things out. No need to respond to anyone. No need to take any action at all. Follow the urge of nothingness. Let yourself have that.

It's time for inaction. Enjoy that. Enjoy the sweet nothing.

You're Allowed To Change Your Boundaries

You've set boundaries. You know your yeses and your nos. But that doesn't mean you have to keep them locked in place just because you set them once.

As you grow and change and as you learn more about yourself, your boundaries are allowed to shift, too. Your yeses might become nos. Your strong no to something might have shifted to a yes.

With time, our wants, needs, and priorities will always evolve, so it is only natural that your boundaries will also evolve.

What worked for you last year, last month, or even yesterday might not work for you today – and that's normal. What didn't work for you in the past might now work for you. That's perfect. Change is a good thing.

Change means you are allowing yourself to grow and that you're being attentive to your present-self. It's time to stop holding onto a past version of you that you're keeping alive just because change can be uncomfortable.

What's more uncomfortable is staying stuck in things that don't feel right anymore.

You're allowed to expand your boundaries, shrink them, move them around, or even tear them down completely if that's what you need. You're not bound by your old decisions and you aren't locked in by the expectations of others. You're allowed to protect yourself in ways that make sense to you now, not in ways that made sense to you then.

You never ever need to apologize for your boundaries. You also don't have to explain them. You don't owe that to anyone.

Changing your boundaries isn't a sign of weakness. It's a sign of self-awareness. It's a sign that you're paying attention to your needs and adjusting accordingly.

The people who respect you will understand that you're doing what's best for you.

Those who push your boundaries, argue with them, and cannot accept them – well, they've given you enough information to know that they are not able to be in your life. That's what boundaries are for.

You have permission to reassess what you will and won't accept in your life. You have the power to choose what feels safe, what feels right, and what allows you to thrive.

You are not locked into your past choices. Keep being attentive to what you need and want. Keep letting yourself rediscover your boundaries.

This is your permission to change your boundaries. Redefine them.

Give yourself permission to take back the power to choose what stays and what goes. You are allowed to change them as often as you need.

It's Okay To
Feel Lost

If you feel lost in your life right now, in what to do, how to move forward, and why you're even here... It's okay that you feel that way. Feeling lost isn't a sign that you're doing something wrong.

It's not the most comfortable feeling, sure, but it is very normal to feel this way. You'll feel this way sometimes. You have felt lost before. Then you found your way. And now, you feel a bit lost again.

It's okay that you feel lost. Whether it's just a fleeting feeling sometimes, or if you've been existing here for a little while.

Not having everything figured out doesn't mean you're failing. It doesn't mean you've taken a wrong turn. It doesn't mean you're doing life "wrong." Feeling lost doesn't mean you are lost.

You might be perfectly positioned and just not able to see it yet. Or maybe you actually are lost, and that isn't a bad thing. Why not embrace being lost?

Feeling lost is a sign that you're in transition, that you're in a space where things are shifting, and that you're in the in-between. That's okay. You're allowed to not know where you're headed and to not have the map in front of you.

Maybe feeling lost really can be a good thing – maybe it'll free you from the idea that you have to follow the set plan and keep playing by the rules and meeting your own expectations.

Can you sense that maybe feeling lost is similar to feeling possibility? It's a slight shift from the discomfort of the uncertain to the *excitement of the unknown.*

But you don't even have to force yourself to feel that, if it's not true. Feeling lost doesn't mean you've lost yourself. It doesn't mean you're broken or that you're falling behind. It doesn't mean that you'll always feel this way.

It's okay to not have the answers right now. It's okay to not see the full picture. Let yourself rest here, in the lost space

Sometimes, the best things come from the times when we feel lost – the moments that force us to stop, to breathe, and to recalibrate. In those moments, we learn to trust ourselves, to lean into the uncertainty, and to embrace the journey, even if it feels scary to sit in the lost-space.

We are often surprised by life and what shows up. We can even find ourselves in ways we didn't even know we wanted to be found.

Feeling lost is just part of finding your way. You'll find your way. You are finding your way. Maybe being lost *is the way right now.*

Your Wounds
Are Lovable

The parts of you that you think are broken, the places inside where you feel the most fragile, and the things that you wish to hide away from the world out of shame – *they are so lovable.* Your wounds are absolutely 100% lovable.

The scars, the pain, the marks left by the hard things you've been through, the parts of yourself that you are still healing, the places within you that you are afraid to look at and for others to see - they don't make you less. They don't take away from your value at all. You are whole, even with all of the wounds.

You don't have to be perfect to be loved. (Plus, it's not possible to be perfect, anyway).You don't have to have it all together to be worthy of love.

You don't need to be better, more healed, more evolved, wiser, fitter, quieter, louder, less big, less curious - nothing. No more or less.

Right now, as you are, without taking anything away or adding anything more, *you are lovable.*

Your wounds don't disqualify you from love; they are simply proof that you are a living, breathing, resilient human that is trying. That is giving life a go. That is here, still showing up despite the difficulties. That is something to be proud of, not something to hide.

And the right people, they will love you, not despite your wounds; their love will extend to your wounds. They will see the role these experiences have played in you becoming who you are; a unique, magical, beautiful being so worthy of love.

You don't need to keep your wounds locked in the dark, tucked away behind a smile. The parts of you that feel raw, that feel tender – they deserve to be seen.

You can let them be seen. You can express them.

It is safe to show your raw, real self. Those parts? They're what make you *you.* They are what make your heart open, your spirit resilient, and your love so deep. They give you empathy for others' wounds, and they let you see the world in a way which gives you a broader perspective. What a superpower. Your wounds have given you this superpower.

Your wounds aren't flaws. They're not imperfections. They are part of you, your story, and your humanity. They make you lovable in ways you haven't even realized yet.

And you are deserving of love, exactly as you are, with all your scars, your imperfections, all your tenderness, and all of those wounds.

Let them be loved. And it starts with you loving them.

It starts with you loving you for all that you are.

It's Okay That Some People Won't Like You

Really, it is. You won't be everyone's favorite person and you don't need to force yourself to be.

There's no need to try to become this ideal version of yourself that somehow everyone will adore so you can finally accept yourself. Other people don't hold the power of your self acceptance.

The truth is, there will be (and already are) people who just don't like you. Whatever their reasoning is, that has nothing to do with you. Even though it seems like it has everything to do with you.

Just because someone really doesn't like choc-mint ice-cream doesn't mean that the ice-cream is existing wrong. Be the choc-mint ice-cream.

Someone not liking you doesn't mean you aren't worthy of being liked. It doesn't mean that you aren't lovable. You're perfectly enough as you are, even if people don't like you.

You don't owe anyone an explanation for being yourself. You don't have to fit into their idea of what's "right" or "acceptable." Some people won't get you. Some people won't gel with your energy.

Some people might even have harsh ideas about you. But it doesn't have to be something you take to heart. It's just how it goes in life, and accepting that simple truth gives you so much more peace than all of the work you're doing to be liked by everyone.

It's easy to get caught up in the need for everyone to like you, to make sure you're accepted, to try and mold yourself into what others want.

It would feel lovely to be loved by every single person you come across, but that expectation really puts a lot of pressure on you. You'll eventually try to become what you think they want, rather than being true to you. That's an exhausting character to maintain.

You're not here to make everyone happy. You're here to be true to *you*, and if that rubs someone the wrong way, that's okay. It doesn't make you any less valuable. And it doesn't mean that they're wrong for not liking you, either.

You not liking bubblegum ice-cream doesn't make you wrong. It just means you have preferences.

People aren't wrong to not like you, just like how it is not wrong for you to not like someone else.

The more you embrace your truth and stop trying so hard to be liked, the more you'll naturally attract the people who get you, who vibe with your energy, and who appreciate you for who you truly are.

The ones who don't will fade away. That's a great thing!

No more shrinking. Hiding. Changing. Controlling. People-Pleasing. *Just let yourself be*. As you are. Whether you're liked or not.

The people who will love you, respect you, and celebrate you for all that you are will be attracted to you showing up as you.

Keep being yourself.

And remember that you're likable, even when you're not liked by everyone.

Take All The Time You Need To Decide

There's no rush. You don't have to have everything figured out in a moment, in a week, or even in a month.

Take the self-imposed deadlines away for the decisions that don't feel ready yet. You can take all the time in the world to decide. There is no need to rush the process.

You can sit on it as long as you need until clarity comes. You don't need to force clarity for anyone else. And not for some expectation you've placed on yourself to just make that decision already.

Give yourself the room to sit in the in-between space of indecision and trust that an answer will make itself known.

You don't owe anyone an instant response or solution. Including yourself. Your life is yours to shape, and you get to move at your own pace. Sometimes, that pace will be a little slower. Sometimes, it'll be a pause.

When you're trying to decide on anything, let the decision come in it's own time, supporting the process by gathering the information you need and not avoiding the work of sitting with it.

That doesn't mean pushing for a decision to come is needed. Do what you can and then allow yourself to rest and wait.

You don't need to force yourself into a decision because you feel pressure or because you feel like you're falling behind. You are allowed to sit with your thoughts and feelings as long as you need until you're certain.

There is power in waiting. There's strength in being willing to take your time and trust that the right answer will come when it's ready. You don't need to rush through the discomfort of uncertainty.

As you sit long enough with the uncertainty, it won't feel as uncomfortable. You might even notice that it feels peaceful to be in the in-between.

Notice if you can touch that space.

You're also allowed to change your mind, to come back to the decision later, and to re-decide. As many times as you wish. There's no shame in taking your time. It's great to be more deliberate and intentional with your decision making.

Take all the time you need. Your life, your decisions, your pace. Give yourself that.

You're Allowed To End Things

Not everything is meant to last forever.

Not every relationship, job, goal, feeling, habit, desire, or chapter in your life will continue on. And that is not only normal, but it is a good thing. Things ending is proof that life is not a stagnant thing. It's proof that you are not stuck in time.

You will grow, change, and adapt. Only always.

As much as you might try to keep something the same, it won't ever be. Time is passing, and every single moment might feel familiar, but it is actually a brand new moment that has never happened before.

When life is changing and you are changing, that means that you will feel the need and desire to end things at times.

Sometimes, the bravest thing you can do is walk away. You don't need to feel guilty for ending a situation that once felt right. You don't need to explain why it's time to let go. Not to anyone. Not even to yourself.

If you feel truthfully that it is time to end something, not because you're running away and avoiding something important, but because it is truly not aligned anymore, then trust that. Honor that truth.

You don't owe anyone an explanation for choosing peace over something that no longer serves you.

Ending things isn't failure. It's not a weakness. It is not disrespectful. Actually, it is the most respectful thing you can do for everyone; to walk away from something that isn't anymore aligned. Not everyone will see it this way, but you know your truth.

Ending things is a sign that you're trusting yourself enough to say, "This isn't working," and then doing what needs to be done to move forward.

You're allowed to let go of friendships that don't bring value and peace to yourself, jobs that exhaust you, environments that stifle your growth.

You don't have to keep holding onto things just because they've been in your life for a while, because you're afraid of disappointing someone, or because it once meant a lot to you.

The right things for you will stay. They will be what you continue with, naturally.

You deserve to end things because you deserve to feel at peace and to be free. You will end more things in the future, too, because later on, there will be other situations that will no longer be aligned with who you are becoming.

As cheesy as it sounds, every ending makes room for a new beginning.

Ending things is a part of living fully, of making choices that serve you and your future, and of respecting and honoring the ever-changing nature of life. Trust that when you let go, you're making space for what's meant to come next.

Give Yourself Forgiveness

No matter what you did, you deserve forgiveness.

You don't have to earn it by proving something to yourself. You don't have to beat yourself up in order to eventually be able to forgive yourself "one day." There's nothing to wait for or to do for you to accept your own forgiveness.

If you are believing that in order to be better; to do better next time, you have to hold it against yourself, let's get something straight: *that's not how growth works.*

You're not alone if you're withholding your forgiveness in hopes of managing your behavior and actions. It's a normal response. It doesn't actually help you grow, though. In many cases, the shame and the regret and critical judgements of yourself only make it worse and keep you stuck in old patterns.

Want to be unstuck? Want to really let yourself learn from your mistakes? Then you absolutely must give yourself the healing balm of forgiveness.

Forgiving yourself helps you to move forward. Forgiving yourself is what will give you the space and peace to be able to create new patterns, and make amends for anything that happened in the past. Whether that requires you to have conversations with others, or simply give yourself some softness, love, and accountability to do your best to keep your promises to yourself in the future.

Forgiveness is not about forgetting or sweeping something under the rug. It's about finally giving yourself the grace to let go.

You don't have to keep holding onto the weight of your past decisions.

You don't deserve that hardness. You don't have to drag the burden of mistakes behind you like a heavy chain, just waiting for you to trip over it again and again. It really doesn't help.

You're allowed to forgive the version of you that didn't know better, that made choices from a place of pain, fear, wounding, or uncertainty.

You're allowed to show that version of you the same kindness you'd show to anyone else struggling. Because the truth is, you are learning, growing, and imperfect.

You will make mistakes, and you will need forgiveness again in the future. Now is the time to start practicing how to give yourself this space and peace.

Forgiveness doesn't erase what happened – it frees you from being bound to it. It gives you permission to stop carrying the past like a shadow over your present. You can learn from what you've been through and let that rest into being as wisdom, without staying stuck there. Wisdom doesn't stay stuck, and it is not born out of this hardness.

The old you doesn't define you. Your growth and your choices now – those are the things that matter. Including the choice to give yourself forgiveness.

The mistakes you made, the things you wish you'd done differently? They don't make you less worthy of love or peace. They don't mean that you are bad, and should be punished and deserve the hard treatment you might sometimes give yourself.

It's time to let go of the "should haves." You don't need to punish yourself anymore. You did what you could with the knowledge you had, and now, you know more. You are more. Let that be enough.

You are allowed to walk your path without the weight of your past dragging behind you.

Forgiving yourself is the way you set yourself free to keep growing, not from force or tension (which doesn't actually work), but from spacious, kind, wise, peaceful love.

You are allowed to heal. You are allowed to move forward. You are allowed to be whole, even with the scars.

Forgive yourself, because you deserve it. You really do. All that is left is for you to accept your own forgiveness.

Like a warm embrace, wrapping your arms around yourself, and letting that healing happen.

You Can Face The Unknown

It's true that the unknown can feel terrifying. It's like an empty void of nothingness. Where we don't know what will happen, how, and when...

This discomfort of the uncertainty often makes us all want to turn away from it. We don't want to face what we don't yet know.

How can we face something we can't see? It's not a lovely feeling to stare at something that isn't clear. Unless, it is...

Unless you could find some lightness in the unknown... Unless you could see what is lovely about staring at a picture that is still being created.

You know what feels good about that? The fact that you are the creator of this picture. You are painting it. You have the brush in your hand, and you can't see the final picture yet because you're still in the process of creating it.

Maybe that is something to be excited about?

It's in the spaces where we don't have all the answers, where we're not sure what's coming next, that we find the greatest opportunities for growth. That we realize that we can create the answer. That not having the answers doesn't mean we have to scramble for clarity where there isn't clarity yet, but that we can rest in the unknown and feel how the creation wants to move through us.

In simple terms, it's about not forcing life to happen because you're afraid that it won't happen in a way that feels good and safe. It's about trusting that just because it is unknown, doesn't mean it won't be safe.

You will keep yourself safe. You will be fine.

You can trust that you can face whatever the unknown reveals, because you are co-creating with the unknown. You won't be a victim of it, you will be the artist.

Of course, you won't have complete control over what happens. And that's a good thing; where the fun in knowing every answer already? Let life surprise you. You can face whatever happens.

Embrace the unknown. Life is messy, unpredictable, and incredibly beautiful. The unknown isn't a monster waiting to trap you. It's a space of possibility.

So many of the greatest moments in life come from stepping into uncertainty. From taking a leap. From walking forward in the darkness with only your trust as the guiding light.

You have the strength, the resilience, and the wisdom to navigate whatever comes your way.

You don't have to know what's ahead. And you don't need to control it. You just need to be open to what comes next.

You're totally capable of being this master artist (because it's what you've already been doing all along).

Tomorrow Is A New Day

Whatever happened today, whatever went right or wrong, whatever you felt, whatever they said, whatever difficulties that came up – it's not permanent.

Tomorrow is a new day. A fresh start. A new chapter.

You just have to claim it.

You don't have to stay stuck where you are. And you won't. Things shift, including your thoughts and feelings.

Let today rest. Tomorrow is yours to create.

It's okay to leave today behind. You don't have to fix everything now, solve all the things, and make it all better in a single day. Tomorrow will come with a clean slate, and it's yours to write on. Fresh energy and a newfound mindset is there for you to drop into.

You have the power within you to not carry today into tomorrow. To wake up and become a new version of yourself.

It is 100% possible. You're not bound by what you have done or who you think you are or should be.

There's power in knowing that you get to decide what tomorrow looks like. While you don't get to decide everything that happens, there is a lot that you do have power over. You have power over your thoughts, the energy you create in your body and connect with, the way you respond to yourself and others, your actions, the mindfulness of being present with what you are doing.

That is all yours.

Tomorrow doesn't need to be perfect, let's take away the pressure of that expectation right now. Tomorrow is a chance to try again, to take a step in the right direction. Holding onto past mistakes and bringing them into tomorrow isn't going to help you not make those mistakes again. That's not how we learn and grow.

You can let it go. Forgive yourself. Forgive others.

If today didn't go the way you hoped, tomorrow gives you the space to try again. You don't need to have it all figured out today or tomorrow. That's not the point.

The point is to know that every single moment is a moment you can begin again. And again. And again.

Begin again as many times as you need. Give yourself that reset. Right now. Tomorrow.

And every tomorrow after that.

And don't forget to keep giving yourself all the loving words you need.

About The Author

Shae Eloise

Shae Eloise is an author, speaker, self-love and worthiness facilitator, mentor, runner, dancer, crochet-nerd, and so much more it's hard for her to remember.

Shae has been working in the world self-development for over a decade, hosting workshops, classes, retreats, mentorships, and courses. She infuses Philosophy, Tao wisdom, Psychology, Internal Family Systems, Inner Child Work, Mindful Self Compassion, and more into her work. Shae is particularly passionate about making self-development accessible, practical, and way less complicated than we believe it is to help people to get free from being hijacked by their wounds.

Shae currently lives in Bali working on new books, teaching dance, leading retreats, and playing hilarious comedy improv games (yes, she's an improv-nerd, too).

Follow Shae online for more information about her upcoming work, books, offerings, courses, retreats, and more.

Visit Shae's Website: www.shaeeloise.com

Visit Shae's Instagram (@shaeeloiseofficial)

Check Out Her Book, Grounded Goddess (For Women)

Made in United States
Cleveland, OH
15 March 2025

15203546R00154